Conten

MW00683110

Nouns
What Is a Noun? 2
Make a Noun Collage 3
What Are Proper Nouns?. 4
Making Nouns Plural 5
Tricky Plural Nouns 6
Nouns Review Quiz 9

Possessive Nouns
Singular Possessive Nouns 11
Plural Possessive Nouns. 12
More Practice with Possessive Nouns 13
Possessive Nouns Review Quiz 15

Pronouns
Pronouns for People 17
Pronouns for Things 18
Possessive Pronouns 19
More Possessive Pronouns 21
Pronouns Review Quiz. 23

Adjectives and Articles
What Is an Adjective? 25
Adjectives Before and After Nouns. 27
Adjectives Can Describe How Many 28
Using Adjectives to Compare Two Things . . 29
Using Adjectives to Compare More Than
    Two Things 30
Tricky Adjectives That Compare 31
Adjectives That Use *More* and *Most*
    to Compare 32
Make an Adjective Poem. 33
Using the Articles *A, An,* and *The* 34
Adjectives and Articles Review Quiz 36

Verbs
What Is a Verb? 38
Make a Verb Collage. 39
The Verbs *Be, Do,* and *Have*. 40
More Practice with *Be, Do,* and *Have* . . . 42
Linking Verbs. 44
Spelling Present Tense Verbs 46
Past Tense Verbs. 47
Spelling Past Tense Verbs 48
Tricky Past Tense Verbs 49
Future Tense Verbs 51
Helping Verbs: Present and Future Tenses . 52
Helping Verbs: Past Tense 54

Subject–Verb Agreement. 56
Pronoun–Verb Agreement 58
Verbs Review Quiz 1 60
Verbs Review Quiz 2 62

Adverbs
Some Adverbs Describe How 64
Some Adverbs Describe When. 65
Some Adverbs Describe Where 66
Some Adverbs Describe How Often 67
Adverbs Review Quiz 68

Sentences and Punctuation
Complete Subjects 70
Complete Predicates 71
What Comes at the End of a Sentence?. . . 72
One Sentence or Two?. 74
Joining Sentences with *And* or *But*. 75
Joining Sentences with *Or* or *So* 76
Sentences and Punctuation Review Quiz . . 77

Contractions and Abbreviations
What Is a Contraction?. 79
More Contractions 80
Abbreviations. 81
Contractions and Abbreviations Review Quiz 83

Special Problems
Using *To, Too,* or *Two* 85
Write the Correct Word. 86
Correcting Errors: "The Lost Mitten" 87
Correcting Errors: "Owls". 88

Vocabulary
Vocabulary List 1. 89
Vocabulary List 1: Review 91
Vocabulary List 2. 92
Vocabulary List 2: Review 94
Vocabulary List 3. 95
Vocabulary List 3: Review 97
Vocabulary List 4. 98
Vocabulary List 4: Review 100
Vocabulary List 5. 101
Vocabulary List 5: Review 103

Grammar Review Test Grade 3 104
Achievement Awards. 110
Answers 111

What Is a Noun?

A **noun** is a word that names a **person**, **place**, or **thing**.

1. Circle the nouns that name a **person**.

   Tom   run   girl   pretty   man   Maria   grandfather   hide   doctor

2. Circle the nouns that name a **place**.

   school   library   small   backyard   eat   falling   mall   beach   Canada

3. Circle the nouns that name a **thing**.

   ask   lamp   pencil   walking   tell   grow   coat   car   tree

4. Circle all the **nouns** in each group of words. Remember that a noun names a **person, place,** or **thing**.

   a) shoe   sing   carrot   basement   quickly

   b) big   teacher   cried   bed   soft

   c) baby   wanted   sister   strong   bedroom

5. Circle the **nouns** in each sentence.

   a) The kitchen is very clean.

   b) Carlos ran quickly down the street.

   c) The truck drove past our house.

   d) Mom painted the bathroom.

6. Write a sentence that has three nouns.

   _____

7. Write a sentence that includes a person and a place.

   _____

8. Write a sentence that includes a person, a place, and a thing.

   _____

Make a Noun Collage

Cut out pictures from magazines and flyers that represent nouns, and paste them below.

What Are Proper Nouns?

Nouns that always begin with a capital letter are called **proper nouns**. The following kinds of nouns always begin with a capital letter:

Specific places, such as a **country, province, city,** or **town.**
Examples: Canada, Manitoba, Brandon

Names of **holidays.**
Example: Canada Day

Names of **people** or **pets.**
Examples: Mr. Brown, Dr. Chong, Fluffy

Names of **days of the week** and **months of the year.**
Examples: Monday, June

1. Use a proper noun to complete each sentence.

a) I would like to visit the province of _____.

b) The first day in January is _____.

c) Halifax, and _____ are Canadian cities.

d) _____ was my teacher in Grade 2.

e) My favourite day of the week is _____.

2. Write eight proper nouns.

_____   _____

_____   _____

_____   _____

_____   _____

Remember to check your writing for proper nouns. Did you use capital letters for all proper nouns?

Canadian Grammar Practice 3 © Chalkboard Publishing

Making Nouns Plural

To make many **nouns** plural, just add the letter **s**.

Examples: rock – rocks   window – windows   flower – flowers

For some nouns, you need to do something different. Watch for nouns like the ones below.

Nouns ending with...	To make the noun plural...
s, **x**, **ch**, or **sh**	Add **es** *Example: one fox – two foxes*
consonant + y	Change the **y** to **i** and add **es** *Example: one fly — two flies*

1. Use **plurals** of the **nouns** below to complete the sentences. Use each noun only once. Choose a noun that makes sense in each sentence.

   wish   dish   match   bunny   box   bush

   a) After dinner, I helped wash the _____.

   b) I saw two _____ in the park today.

   c) My mother planted two _____ in the backyard.

   d) Pablo packed his books into two _____.

   e) In the fairy tale, the girl got to make three _____.

   f) Dad used _____ to light the candles on the cake.

2. Rewrite each sentence to make the underlined nouns **plural**. **Do not** use the words **a** or **an** before a plural noun.

   a) I got a <u>scratch</u> on my <u>arm</u>.

   _____

   b) I saw a <u>lady</u> wearing a <u>dress</u>.

   _____

Tricky Plural Nouns

Making some nouns plural is tricky!
Be careful when making plurals from nouns that end with the letter **o**.
For some nouns that end with **o**, add the letters **es**.
For other nouns that end with **o**, just add the letter **s**.

Add *es*	Add *s*	
echo – echoes hero – heroes potato – potatoes tomato – tomatoes	patio – patios photo – photos piano – pianos radio – radios	video – videos zero – zeros

1. Complete each sentence below by writing a **plural noun** from the lists above.

   Choose a word that makes sense in the sentence.

   a) The restaurant has two _____ where people eat outside.

   b) There are two _____ in the number 100.

   c) We picked the _____ that were red and ripe.

   d) All _____ have black keys and white keys.

2. Rewrite each sentence below to make the underlined nouns **plural**. **Do not** use the words *a* or *an* before a plural noun.

   a) The <u>hero</u> turned on a <u>radio</u> to hear the news.

   _____

   b) Larry sent me a <u>photo</u> of a <u>potato</u> from his garden.

   _____

   c) In the <u>video</u>, people heard an <u>echo</u>.

   _____

   Canadian Grammar Practice 3 © Chalkboard Publishing

Tricky Plural Nouns (continued)

Watch out when making plurals from nouns that end with the letter **f**.
For most nouns that end with *f*, change the *f* to a *v* and add *es*.
For a few nouns that end with *f*, just add the letter *s*.

Change *f* to *v* and add *es*		Just add *s*
elf – elves	scarf – scarves	chef – chefs
half – halves	shelf – shelves	cliff – cliffs
leaf – leaves	thief – thieves	roof – roofs
loaf – loaves	wolf – wolves	sheriff – sheriffs

3. Complete the sentences below by writing a **plural noun** from the lists above. Choose a word that makes sense in each sentence.

   a) You can share an apple by cutting it into two _____.

   b) The _____ stole many bicycles.

   c) Three _____ howled loudly during the night.

   d) The library has many _____ full of books.

4. Rewrite each sentence to make the underlined nouns **plural**. **Do not** use the words *a* or *an* before a plural noun.

   a) The <u>chef</u> made a <u>loaf</u> of bread.

   _____

   b) A <u>leaf</u> blew onto the <u>roof</u>.

   _____

   c) It is dangerous to play near a <u>cliff</u>.

   _____

   d) The <u>sheriff</u> caught a <u>thief</u>.

   _____

Tricky Plural Nouns (continued)

Do not be tricked by tricky **plural nouns**!

For nouns ending with the letters *fe*, change the *f* to a *v* and add *s*.
Examples: knife – knives   life – lives   wife – wives

To make these nouns plural, do not change anything!
Examples: one fish – two fish   one sheep – six sheep   one deer – four deer

You will need to remember the tricky plurals below.

Singular	Plural
child	children
foot	feet
goose	geese

Singular	Plural
mouse	mice
person	people
tooth	teeth

5. Complete each sentence by writing a **plural noun** from the lists above.

   a) My father uses _____ to cut vegetables for dinner.

   b) When we went fishing, my sister caught three _____.

   c) I like to learn about the _____ of famous people.

   d) The three woolly _____ ran away.

6. Rewrite these sentences to make the underlined nouns **plural**. **Do not** use the words *a* or *an* before a plural noun.

   a) The <u>wife</u> made lots of food for the party.

   _____

   b) A <u>mouse</u> ran over my <u>foot</u>!

   _____

   c) The <u>child</u> fed the <u>goose</u>.

   _____

   d) The <u>woman</u> saw a <u>deer</u> in the woods.

   _____

Nouns Review Quiz

1. Complete the sentences about **nouns**.

   a) A noun can name a _____, _____, or _____.

   b) A _____ noun is a noun that always begins with a capital letter.

2. Underline all the **nouns** in each sentence.

   a) Mom put your mittens on the top shelf in the closet.

   b) Bees and butterflies visit the flowers in our backyard.

   c) The mountains in British Columbia are amazing to see!

   d) The nurse gave the doctor some papers to read.

   e) If the windows are closed, how did a bird get in the house?

   f) Darnell went to the beach with some friends.

3. Change the first letter in **proper nouns** to a capital letter.

   a) I saw mrs. greenway at the mall last tuesday.

   b) My dog rover is coming to nova scotia with us.

   c) Will dr. conway come to dinner on labour day?

   d) Is toronto one of the largest cities in canada?

   e) I think uncle alfred will spend the winter in florida.

   f) Every year, valentine's day is on february 14.

4. Write the **plural** of each noun.

a) box _____

b) person _____

c) video _____

d) lunch _____

e) key _____

f) tomato _____

g) baby _____

h) wolf _____

i) deer _____

j) mouse _____

k) brush _____

l) shelf _____

m) knife _____

n) goose _____

5. In each sentence, circle the correct **possessive noun**.

a) Your (sleefs   sleeves) are worn out at the elbows.

b) My friends came over to watch some new (videoes   videos) with me.

c) The parents watched the (children   childrens) perform their play.

d) My voice (echoes   echos) when I yell into the cave.

e) That squirrel has run across all the (rooves   roofs) on my street.

f) The dentist said my (tooths   teeth) are in great shape.

g) I would like some (tomatoes   tomatos) in my salad, please.

h) The (ponys   ponies) raced each other around the field.

Singular Possessive Nouns

A **possessive noun** shows who or what something belongs to. Add an **apostrophe** (') + *s* to a **singular noun** to show belonging. Below are two examples of **singular possessive nouns**.

	Singular Possessive Nouns
the coat that belongs to my father	*my **father's** coat*
the mittens that belong to Carla	***Carla's** mittens*

1. Write the **singular possessive noun** for each example below.

   a) the shoes that belong to Amira   _____ shoes

   b) the nest that belongs to the bird   the _____ nest

   c) the marbles that belong to Omar   _____ marbles

   d) the scarf that belongs to the woman   the _____ scarf

2. Rewrite each sentence. Use a **singular possessive noun** to replace the underlined words in each sentence.

   Example: He painted the legs of the table.
   *He painted the **table's** legs.*

   a) Mario turned the pages of the book.

   _____

   b) The handle of the mug broke off.

   _____

   c) The leaves of the plant turned brown.

   _____

Plural Possessive Nouns

Most **plural nouns** end with *s*. Add an **apostrophe (')** **after the *s*** to make a **plural possessive noun**. Below are some examples.

	Plural Possessive Nouns
the hats that belong to the girls	*the **girls'** hats*
the barking of the dogs	*the **dogs'** barking*
the leaves of the trees	*the **trees'** leaves*

Some **plural nouns** do not end with *s*.
Examples: children   women   men   people

Add an **apostrophe (')** + *s* to turn these plural nouns into **plural possessive nouns**.
Examples: children's   women's   men's   people's

1. Write the **plural possessive noun** for each example below.

   a) the coats that belong to my sisters   my _____ coats

   b) the cat that belongs to my cousins   my _____ cat

   c) the honking of the cars   the _____ honking

   d) the roars of the lions   the _____ roars

2. Write the **plural possessive noun** for each example below.

   a) the laughter of the people   the _____ laughter

   b) the toys belonging to the children   the _____ toys

   c) the gloves belonging to the men   the _____ gloves

   d) the bikes belonging to the women   the _____ bikes

More Practice with Possessive Nouns

Use a **possessive noun** to show who or what something belongs to. Change a **singular** noun into a **possessive** noun by adding an **apostrophe** (') **+ s**. Look at the examples in the chart below.

Singular Noun	Possessive Noun	Example Sentence
Anne	Anne**'s**	**Anne's** new glasses look nice.
dog	dog**'s**	The **dog's** paws are muddy.
car	car**'s**	The **car's** horn is very loud!

1. Rewrite each sentence. Use a **singular possessive noun.** Look at the examples below.

   Examples: The handle <u>of the cup</u> is broken.   I like the kitten <u>that belongs to Tim</u>.
   The cup's handle is broken.   I like Tim's kitten.

   a) The front tire <u>of my bike</u> is flat.

   _____

   b) Please give me the phone number <u>of the store</u>.

   _____

   c) Did you find the pencil <u>that belongs to Suki</u>?

   _____

   d) This is the watch <u>that belongs to my father</u>.

   _____

   e) The feet <u>of the elephant</u> are huge!

   _____

More Practice with Possessive Nouns (continued)

How do you change a **plural noun** into a **possessive** noun?
If the **plural** noun ends with an **s**, add an **apostrophe** (').
If the **plural** noun does **not** end with an **s**, add an **apostrophe** (') **+ s**.
Look at the examples in the chart below.

Plural Noun	Possessive Noun	Example Sentence
sisters	sisters'	My **sisters'** shoes got wet in the rain.
children	children's	The **children's** parents are coming.

2. Rewrite each sentence. Use a **plural possessive noun.** Look at the examples below.

Examples:
I found the hats <u>that belong to the men</u>.   *The windows <u>of the cars</u> are dirty.*
I found the men's hats.   *The cars' windows are dirty.*

a) The leaves <u>of the trees</u> change colour in the fall.

_____

b) The lids <u>of the jars</u> are in the top drawer.

_____

c) The cars <u>that belong to the people</u> are parked outside.

_____

d) The coats <u>that belong to my brothers</u> are in the closet.

_____

e) We could hear the voices <u>of the women</u>.

_____

Possessive Nouns Review Quiz

1. In each sentence, circle the correct **possessive noun**. Think about whether the sentence needs a **singular** or **plural** possessive noun.

   a) This (shirt's shirts') sleeves are too short for me.

   b) I put away the (puppy's puppies') toys while they were playing outside.

   c) The (children's childrens') teacher taught them a new song.

   d) Dad found (Kim's Kims') mittens on the floor of the hall closet.

   e) Both my (shoe's shoes') laces had come untied.

   f) My baseball (team's teams') uniforms are green and white.

   g) (Kayla's Kaylas') brothers told us some funny jokes.

2. Read each sentence and underline each **possessive noun**. If the possessive noun is **correct**, put a check mark above it. If it is **not correct**, cross it out and write the correct possessive noun above it.

   a) The plant's leaves turned brown when we forgot to water them.

   b) This bird's feathers will get darker when it is older.

   c) My parents met Liams' parents at the school play.

   d) My two sister's eyes are blue, and my eyes are brown.

   e) Jeremy's sweater got caught in his coats' zipper.

   f) The womens' team played first, and the men's team played next.

   g) The markers' caps show what colour ink is inside.

Possessive Nouns Review Quiz (continued)

3. Circle the correct **singular possessive noun** in each sentence.

a) My (aunt's   aunts') fingernails were painted all different colours.

b) That twisted stick is the (monkeys'   monkey's) favourite toy.

c) Our (dogs'   dog's) chew bones are buried in the yard.

d) My (cat's   cats') hairs are all over my pants.

e) (Jim's   Jims') books are all packed in boxes now.

f) The (girl's   girls') hair was shiny after she brushed it.

g) The racing (teams'   team's) helmets matched their clothing.

4. Write the **plural possessive noun** for each example below.

a) the toys belonging to the children   the _____ toys

b) the badges earned by the Scouts   the _____ badges

c) the songs of the women   the _____ songs

d) the shapes of the clouds   the _____ shapes

e) the voices of the people   the _____ voices

f) the shirts of the men   the _____ shirts

g) the bikes belonging to the racers   the _____ bikes

Canadian Grammar Practice 3 © Chalkboard Publishing

Pronouns for People

A **pronoun** is a word that takes the place of one or more nouns.
Use these pronouns to take the place of nouns that name **people**.

I   you   he   she   we   they   him   her   them   us

1. Use a **pronoun** to take the place of the underlined word or words.

   a) <u>Ralph</u> likes horses.

   _____ likes horses.

   b) <u>The children</u> played hide and seek.

   _____ played hide and seek.

   c) Emma shared the grapes with <u>Eva and Ravi</u>.

   Emma shared the grapes with _____.

2. Rewrite each sentence. Change the underlined word or words to a **pronoun**.

   a) <u>Jack and Ana</u> played with the puppies.

   _____

   b) <u>Lu</u> showed the picture to <u>Marc</u>.

   _____

   c) <u>The doctor and the nurse</u> smiled at <u>my sister and me</u>.

   _____

   d) <u>Tanya and I</u> waved goodbye to <u>our aunt and uncle</u>.

   _____

Pronouns for Things

A **pronoun** is a word that takes the place of one or more nouns.

Pronouns take the place of nouns that name **people, places,** or **things.**

Use the pronouns below to take the place of nouns that name **things.**

it they them

1. Use a **pronoun** to take the place of the words in brackets.

   a) Andrew was reading _____. (the book)

   b) _____ are bending in the wind. (The trees)

   c) I found _____ behind the chair. (my mittens)

   d) _____ have pictures of animals. (The stickers)

2. Rewrite the sentences to use pronouns for **people** and **things.** Change the underlined word or words to a **pronoun.**

   a) The girls gave the toys to San and me.

   _____

   b) The boxes are too big for Alan and Rosa to carry.

   _____

   c) Dave and I sent the birthday card to our grandfather.

   _____

   d) Will Amit and Brittany sing for the visitors?

   _____

Canadian Grammar Practice 3 © Chalkboard Publishing

Possessive Pronouns

A **pronoun** takes the place of a **noun**. Look at the sentences below.

Example: <u>Angela</u> waved to <u>Sami</u>. (Angela and Sami are nouns).
     <u>She</u> waved to <u>him</u>.

She and *him* are **pronouns** that take the place of nouns.

A **possessive pronoun** takes the place of a **possessive noun**.
A **possessive pronoun** shows who or what something belongs to.

Example: Ricardo is <u>Anna's</u> cousin. (Anna's is a possessive noun.)
     Ricardo is <u>her</u> cousin.

Her is a **possessive pronoun** that takes the place of *Anna's*.

Use the **possessive pronouns** below before nouns.

my   your   his   her   its   our   their

1. Circle the **possessive pronouns**. Remember that a possessive pronoun shows who or what something belongs to.

   a) Eva said, "This loud noise is hurting my ears!"

   b) The wind blew the hat off his head.

   c) The two birds flew back to their nest in the tree.

   d) "Is your mother home from work yet?" asked Mrs. Winters.

   e) My brother and I take our shoes off when we go in the house.

   f) This sweater is missing two of its buttons.

   g) Linda put the notebook in her backpack.

   h) Our neighbours are going to sell their house.

Possessive Pronouns (continued)

2. Rewrite each sentence. Replace the underlined **possessive noun** with a **possessive pronoun**.

a) Frank scratched <u>Frank's</u> nose because it was itchy.

_____

b) We are going to have dinner at <u>Aunt Selma's</u> house.

_____

c) The Smiths saw birds eating from <u>the Smiths'</u> bird feeder.

_____

d) <u>The clock's</u> batteries are dead.

_____

e) "Emilio, is it <u>Emilio's</u> birthday today?" Gary asked.

_____

f) The teachers said, "It is <u>the teachers'</u> job to help you learn."

_____

g) Gail said, "You can borrow <u>Gail's</u> eraser."

_____

h) The toy truck is missing one of <u>the truck's</u> wheels.

_____

More Possessive Pronouns

Sometimes, **possessive pronouns** do **not** come before a noun. Look at the examples below.

Example: This book is <u>my book</u>.

The possessive pronoun *my* comes before the noun *book*.

Example: This book is <u>mine</u>.

Mine is a **possessive pronoun** that takes the place of *my book*.
Mine does not come before a noun.

Example: I drank my milk, but Sasha did not drink <u>her milk</u>.
      I drank my milk, but Sasha did not drink <u>hers</u>.
Hers is a **possessive pronoun** that takes the place of *her milk*.

Hers does not come before a noun.

The possessive pronouns below **do not** have to come before a noun.

mine   yours   his   hers   ours   theirs

1. Underline the **possessive pronouns** that come **before** a noun. Circle the **possessive pronouns** that **do not** come before a noun.

   a) I asked Amit if this is his mitten. He said, "It is not mine."

   b) Gail finished writing her story, but Julio is still writing his.

   c) Todd and Leanne both drew pictures of bears. "Yours is just as nice as hers," the teacher told Todd.

   d) Dad liked the colour the neighbours painted their house. "We should paint ours the same colour as theirs," he said.

   e) Emma and Andrew have toy robots. Hers makes sounds and his has flashing lights.

Did you notice which possessive pronoun in these questions sometimes comes before a noun and sometimes does not? Which one is it?

More Possessive Pronouns (continued)

2. Rewrite each sentence. Replace the underlined words with the correct **possessive pronoun**.

   a) My brother's feet are bigger than <u>my feet</u>.

   _____

   b) Our dog barks louder than <u>their dog</u>.

   _____

   c) I think your joke is funnier than <u>John's joke</u>.

   _____

   d) Are these <u>Mom's keys</u> or <u>Dad's keys</u>?

   _____

3. Circle the correct **possessive pronoun** in the brackets.

   a) We think (our ours) team is better than (their theirs).

   b) (Your Yours) sweater has stripes, and (my mine) does, too!

   c) (My Mine) pen ran out of ink, so may I borrow (your yours)?

   d) My uncle grows beautiful roses in his garden, and we grow vegetables in
      (our ours).

   e) My sister's bedroom is bigger than (my mine), but I like (my mine) better than
      (her hers).

   f) Is (your yours) apartment on a higher floor than (their theirs)?

 Canadian Grammar Practice 3 © Chalkboard Publishing

Pronouns Review Quiz

1. Rewrite each sentence. Use a **pronoun** to replace each **underlined word** or **group of words**.

a) My name is Eddie, and <u>Eddie</u> can help you.

_____

b) <u>My friends and I</u> worked hard on our project.

_____

c) Please put <u>the ice cubes</u> in the freezer.

_____

d) <u>The girls</u> gave <u>Peter</u> a birthday card.

_____

e) <u>Sally</u> has already returned <u>the books</u> to <u>Tony and me</u>.

_____

f) <u>The shoes</u> are too big for <u>Emma</u>.

_____

g) <u>This book</u> is not too hard for <u>the boys</u> to read.

_____

h) <u>Marco</u> gave one apple to each of <u>the children</u>.

_____

Pronouns Review Quiz (continued)

2. In each sentence, write the correct **possessive pronoun** to replace the word or words in brackets.

   a) _____ new radio is on the kitchen table. (Uncle Harry's)

   b) I see _____ writing on _____ pages. (Mom's; the book's)

   c) Can we give the cats _____ (the cats') food now?

   d) Ken said, "_____ (Ken's) bicycle has a flat tire!"

   e) _____ (My sister's and my) feet are sore from walking so far.

   f) I told Ping, "_____ (Ping's) socks are very colourful!"

   g) All _____ (the trees') branches are covered with flowers.

3. Rewrite each sentence. Replace the **underlined words** with a **possessive pronoun**.

   a) Your legs are longer than my legs.

   _____

   b) His frog can jump farther than her frog.

   _____

   c) Our apartment is on a higher floor than their apartment.

   _____

   d) Her bedroom is messier than my bedroom.

   _____

Canadian Grammar Practice 3 © Chalkboard Publishing

What Is an Adjective?

An **adjective** is a word that describes a noun.

Example: A big lion ran after me!

The word *big* is an adjective. It describes the noun *lion*.

1. Circle the **adjective** in each sentence. Underline the **noun** it describes.

   a) A brown mouse ran over the carpet.

   b) Mr. Tanaka gave me a large book.

   c) A scary dragon lived in the cave.

   d) The playful puppy ran after me.

   e) Please pass me the green mug.

   f) I fell on the slippery ice.

   g) The loud thunder woke me up.

   h) She watched an interesting movie with Jack.

   i) Carol told me a funny joke.

   j) They put the presents on the round table.

   k) I want to climb a tall mountain.

   l) Bob washed the dirty dishes.

   m) Rachel walked down the lonely road.

   n) The rabbit leaped through the tall grass.

   o) Dave did his happy dance.

   p) The colourful pigeons cooed softly.

   q) The angry cat chased our dog.

What Is an Adjective? (continued)

2. In each sentence below, write an **adjective** that makes sense. Underline the **noun** your adjective describes.

a) I think I will wear the _____ socks today.

b) Pedro spoke in a _____ voice.

c) There were _____ clouds in the sky.

d) A _____ runner will win the race.

e) Dad put the _____ flowers in a vase.

f) The _____ cat chased a mouse.

g) The _____ dog did not move when Mom swept.

3. Circle the **adjective** in brackets that fits best.

a) Wanda put a (round   heavy) book in her backpack.

b) The (yellow   warm) fire melted the snow on her clothes.

c) The (bright   loud) lightning lit up the room.

d) The author had some (great   old) ideas for a new book.

e) Tom left his (worst   favourite) pen at school today.

f) The (sleepy   striped) cat curled up in the (yellow   warm) sunshine.

g) The (pretty   dim) lights sparkled in the (cold   dark) night.

Adjectives Before and After Nouns

An **adjective** describes a noun. Sometimes an adjective comes **before** the noun it describes. Sometimes the adjective comes **after** the noun.

Examples: **Before a noun:** *We walked across the (shiny) floor.*

   After a noun: *The floor was (shiny.)*

1. Circle the **adjective** in each sentence. Underline the **noun** it describes.

   a) The clown was funny.

   b) Do not cross the street when the light is red.

   c) The woman was angry when the dog chased a cat.

   d) Do you think the towels are dry?

   e) The video Ali watched was exciting.

   f) The pillow I sleep on is soft.

   g) The baby in the crib is cute.

   h) Mr. Rossi makes sandwiches that are delicious.

   i) I wear sunglasses when the sun is bright.

   j) We did not go swimming because the water was cold.

   k) Enzo was tired after he played soccer.

   l) Mrs. Jones told me that the answer is correct.

2. Circle each **adjective** and underline each **noun**. Draw an arrow from each adjective to the noun it describes.

   Example: The (old) man wore a scarf that was (yellow.)

   a) The huge dinosaur had teeth that were sharp.

   b) The children were happy when the colourful rainbow appeared.

   c) A woman who was tall fixed our leaky roof.

Adjectives Can Describe How Many

An **adjective** describes a noun. Some adjectives answer the question "How many?" **Numbers** can be adjectives.

Example: I popped three balloons!

In this sentence, *three* is an **adjective** that describes the noun **balloons**.
The adjective *three* answers the question "How many balloons?"

Some **adjectives** answer the question "How many?" but they do not tell exactly how many.

Example: I have some questions for you.

In this sentence, *some* is an **adjective** that describes the noun *questions. Some* does not tell exactly how many questions, but it tells us there are more than one.

1. Circle the **adjectives** and underline **all** the **nouns**. Draw an arrow from each adjective to the **noun it describes**.

   a) Three apples fell from the tree.

   b) Raj found four coins under the bed.

   c) Sandra watched two squirrels climb a tree.

   d) Eight frogs hopped into the pond.

2. Circle each **adjective** that answers the question "How many?"

   a) I returned several books to the library.

   b) Many students are absent today.

   c) Few people keep snakes as pets.

   d) We watched some airplanes land at the airport.

   e) There were many cows on the farm, but I saw few horses.

   f) I have collected several seashells and many rocks.

Using Adjectives to Compare Two Things

You can use an **adjective** to **compare two things**.

Example: Sam is <u>taller</u> than Ali.

This sentence compares how tall Sam and Ali are.

For many adjectives that have **one syllable**, just add *er* to make an adjective that compares two things.

Examples: fast – faster   short – shorter

For these adjectives, double the **final consonant** before adding *er*.

hot – hotter   big – bigger   fat – fatter   sad – sadder

1. Complete each sentence. Change the **adjective** in brackets to make it **compare two things**.

   a) My brother is _____ than my sister. (old)

   b) The green book is _____ than the red book. (thick)

   c) A dime is _____ than a quarter. (small)

   d) January is _____ than June. (cold)

   e) The sun is _____ than the moon. (bright)

   f) The kitchen is _____ than the basement. (warm)

   g) My new pillow is _____ than my old pillow. (soft)

2. Complete each sentence. Change the **adjective** in brackets to make it **compare two things**.

   a) Henry was _____ than Tina when it was time to go. (sad)

   b) Today is _____ than yesterday. (hot)

   c) My cat is _____ than your cat. (fat)

   d) A truck is _____ than a car. (big)

Using Adjectives to Compare More Than Two Things

You can use adjectives to compare **more than two things**.

Example: Anna is the tallest student in the class.

This sentence **compares** all the students in the class. Anna is the tallest.

For most adjectives that have one syllable, add **est** to make an adjective that compares **more than two things**.

Example: short – shortest

1. Use the **adjective** in brackets to complete the first sentence in each pair. Use the correct form of the adjective to compare **more than two things**. Then complete the second sentence to tell what is being compared.

   a) Lily was the _____ runner in the race. (fast)

      This sentence compares all the _____.

   b) Today is the _____ day of the year. (cold)

      This sentence compares all the _____.

   c) This is the _____ coat in my closet. (warm)

      This sentence compares _____ in my closet.

   d) My bed is the _____ bed in the house. (soft)

      This sentence compares _____ in the house.

2. Use the **adjective** in brackets to compare **more than two things**. Remember to write **the** before an adjective that ends with **est.**

   a) The red truck is _____ truck in the garage. (clean)

   b) This light bulb is _____ light bulb we have. (bright)

   c) The dictionary is _____ book on the shelf. (thick)

   d) I took _____ muffin on the plate. (small)

Canadian Grammar Practice 3 © Chalkboard Publishing

Tricky Adjectives That Compare

Watch out for these tricky adjectives that compare!

Adjective	To Compare Two Things	To Compare More Than Two Things
good	better	best
bad	worse	worst
far	farther	farthest
many	more	most

Use the **adjective** in brackets to complete the first sentence in the pair. Then circle the correct answer in the second sentence. Write *the* before an adjective that compares **more than two things**.

a) The story about dragons was _____ than the story about dinosaurs. (good)

This sentence compares (two things   more than two things).

b) Do you think a sore throat is _____ than a cough? (bad)

This sentence compares (two things   more than two things).

c) Hockey and baseball are good, but I think soccer is _____ sport. (good)

This sentence compares (two things   more than two things).

d) Your house is _____ from school than my house. (far)

This sentence compares (two things   more than two things).

e) Of all the classes in our school, Mr. Rico's class has _____ students. (many)

This sentence compares (two things   more than two things).

f) There were some bad storms last year, but this storm is _____. (bad)

This sentence compares (two things   more than two things).

Adjectives That Use *More* and *Most* to Compare

For most adjectives that have **two or more syllables**, use *more* to compare **two things**. Use *the most* to compare **more than two things**.

Compare Two Things	Compare More Than Two Things
Karen is <u>more</u> helpful than Bill.	*Johnny is <u>the most</u> helpful of all the children in the class.*

Watch out for adjectives that have **two** syllables, and **end with y**. For these adjectives, change the **y** to **i** and add **er** or **est** when you want to compare.

Examples: shiny – shinier – shiniest   easy – easier – easiest
hungry – hungrier – hungriest   healthy – healthier – healthiest

1. Read each sentence and think about how many things are compared. Complete the sentence by writing *more* or *the most.*

   a) Liz was frightened, but Larry was _____ frightened.

   b) We saw elephants and giraffes, but I thought the monkeys were _____ interesting animals at the zoo.

   c) Bob thinks apples are _____ delicious than bananas.

   d) Of all the women at the ball, Prince Charming thought Cinderella was

   _____ beautiful.

2. Use the correct form of the word in brackets to compare. Remember to use *the* with words ending in *est*.

   a) The old tabby cat is _____ cat in the neighbourhood. (grumpy)

   b) Cindy's dog is _____ than my dog. (hairy)

   c) Today, my brother is acting _____ he's ever acted. (silly)

   d) That sheep has _____ coat I've ever seen. (curly)

Make an Adjective Poem

Cut out and paste a picture of a person, place, or thing from a magazine onto the middle of the space below. Write adjectives around the picture to describe what you have chosen and to create a poem. The first word in the poem should name the person, place, or thing you have chosen.

Using the Articles *A*, *An*, and *The*

The words *a*, *an*, and *the* are called **articles**. Use *a* before a **singular noun** that starts with a **consonant**. Use *an* before a **singular noun** that starts with a **vowel**. Look at the examples below.

Examples: *a* monkey   *a* river   *a* washer
           an eel   *an* arrow   *an* octopus

Use *the* before a **singular** or **plural noun**.

Examples: *the* pipe   *the* dress   *the* snakes   *the* elephants

Choosing Between *A*, *An*, and *The*

Use *the* when you are talking about something **specific**. A specific thing is **one particular example**.

Example: <u>***The*** car</u> *parked on the road does not belong to us.*

This sentence is not about just any car. It is about one particular example of a car—the car that is parked on the road. The writer used *the* to talk about a **specific** car.

A **specific** example can include **more than one** thing.

Example: <u>***The*** sailboats</u> *we saw at the marina were beautiful.*

This sentence is not about just any sailboats. It is about the particular sailboats the writer saw at the marina. The writer used *the* to talk about a **specific** example of a group of sailboats.

Use *a* or *an* when you are talking about something **in general**. That means you are **not** talking about a **specific** example.

Example: *We went to the animal shelter to adopt* <u>***a*** puppy</u>.

The writer is talking about a puppy **in general**. There is **not** one specific example of a puppy that the writer has already seen and has decided to get.

Example: *We went to the animal shelter to adopt* <u>***the*** puppy</u> *we saw there yesterday.*

This sentence is about a **specific** example of a puppy, so the writer used *the* instead of *a*.

Canadian Grammar Practice 3 © Chalkboard Publishing

Using the Articles *A*, *An*, and *The* (continued)

Sometimes, a **singular noun** has an **adjective** in front of it. If the sentence is **not** talking about a **specific** example and the adjective starts with a **vowel**, use *an*.

Examples: ***an*** *old book* ***an*** *easy puzzle* ***an*** *interesting idea*

If the **singular noun** is **not** a specific example and the **adjective** starts with a **consonant**, use *a* even if the noun starts with a vowel.

Examples: ***a*** *happy child* ***a*** *blue ball* ***a*** *frisky dog*

Write the correct word (*a, an,* or *the*) in each sentence. Think about whether the sentence is about something **specific** or something **general**.

a) We are all excited about visiting my cousins at _____ cottage.

b) There is _____ beaver on the Canadian nickel.

c) When we go to the zoo, I always want to see _____ elephants.

d) I read that _____ emu is taller than my father.

e) _____ baby's blanket was all wet.

f) Jeff rides _____ bicycle in _____ park.

g) My sister wants _____ apple and I want _____ pear.

h) I can spin _____ nickel, but I cannot spin _____ dime.

i) Cara drew _____ picture of _____ apple tree.

j) Tim went to _____ park to play on _____ swings.

k) _____ squirrel that lives in our tree made _____ pile of acorns under _____ oak tree.

l) I went to _____ library to return _____ book I borrowed last week.

m) _____ bear walked into _____ woods and ate _____ amazing amount of berries.

Adjectives and Articles Review Quiz

1. Circle each **adjective** and underline each **noun**. Draw an arrow from each **adjective** to the **noun** it describes.

   a) The old man lived in a big house beside a beautiful lake.

   b) The wet floor was slippery.

   c) The soup is hot and delicious.

   d) Two women sat in chairs under a tall tree.

   e) Many children like funny stories better than scary stories.

   f) Several people brought some snacks to the party.

   g) Few guests came late, and four people came early.

   h) The little boy with red hair is tired.

2. In each sentence, circle the correct way to use **adjectives** to compare.

   a) Taylor swims fast, but Jenny swims (faster the fastest).

   b) The children in the choir sang loud, but Tim sang (louder the loudest).

   c) These two snakes are long, but the green one is (longer the longest).

   d) Mom and I both have short hair, but my hair is (shorter the shortest).

   e) Of all the children on my team, Kyle is (taller the tallest).

   f) Tom and Leah are hungry, but I am (hungrier the hungriest).

   g) My two sisters are funny, but my older sister is (funnier the funniest).

3. In each sentence, circle the correct way to **compare** two or more things.

   a) Roberto was frightened, but his sister was (more the most) frightened.

   b) I tasted three soups, and the chicken soup was (more the most) delicious.

   c) The book has seven chapters, and the last chapter is (more the most) interesting.

   d) My dad's garden and my grandmother's garden are both beautiful, but my grandmother's garden is (more the most) beautiful.

   e) I have seen many movies, but this movie is (more the most) exciting one I have ever seen.

   f) The second question on the quiz is (more the most) difficult than the first question.

4. Complete the sentences with the correct word—*a*, *an*, or *the*.

   a) The Millers hope to buy _____ house somewhere near a lake.

   b) Let us see if the library has _____ book this movie is based on.

   c) I want to find a place where I can buy _____ sandwich for lunch.

   d) Do you have _____ extra pencil I can borrow?

   e) He needs to buy _____ light bulb to put in this lamp.

   f) I have one sock, but I do not know where _____ matching one is.

   g) When we go to Africa, we hope to see _____ elephant.

What Is a Verb?

A **verb** is a word that tells what someone or something is doing.
In the sentences below, the verbs are underlined.

Examples: Karen <u>reaches</u> for the book.   The glass <u>falls</u> to the floor.

1. Circle the **verb** in each sentence.

   a) Justin jumps over the puddle.

   b) The bird flies far away.

   c) Eliza gives an apple to her sister.

   d) Lightning flashes across the sky.

   e) He forgets my name all the time.

   f) My grandmother sends me a birthday card every year.

   g) I see a nest in that tree!

   h) That door squeaks when you open it.

   i) Carla and Frank dance to the music.

   j) The happy sheep runs down the hill.

2. Circle the all the **verbs** in each group of words.

   a) wood   rug   tells   spiders   cleans

   b) writes   pencil   erasers   penny   says

   c) builds   roads   explores   garbage   tea

   d) windows   sports   hears   hides   bush

   e) buys   medicine   rainbows   scarf   pours

   f) remembers   pillows   asks   scrubs   suitcase

   g) skips   sidewalk   decides   kittens   shoes

Make a Verb Collage

Cut out pictures from magazines and flyers that represent verbs, and paste them below.

The Verbs *Be*, *Do*, and *Have*

Below are the **present tense** forms of the verbs *be*, *do*, and *have*.

Be	Do	Have
*I **am***	*I **do***	*I **have***
*he **is**, she **is**, it **is***	*he **does**, she **does**, it **does***	*he **has**, she **has**, it **has***
*we **are**, you **are**, they **are***	*we **do**, you **do**, they **do***	*we **have**, you **have**, they **have***

1. Write the correct **present tense** form of the verb **be**.

   a) It _____ amazing that you got here so quickly.

   b) They _____ sad that they will not be able to come with us.

   c) I _____ sure I will score a goal in the game tonight.

   d) You _____ very lucky to have such a good friend.

2. Write the correct **present tense** form of the verb **do**.

   a) We _____ not drop litter on the ground.

   b) He always _____ his homework after supper.

   c) Sometimes, I _____ exercises to help me stay fit.

   d) It _____ a good job of vacuuming up dirt and dust.

3. Write the correct **present tense** form of the verb **have**.

   a) They _____ seven fish in their aquarium.

   b) I _____ long red hair and blue eyes.

   c) She _____ a pencil case just like mine.

   d) You _____ some very interesting ideas!

Canadian Grammar Practice 3 © Chalkboard Publishing

The Verbs *Be, Do,* and *Have* (continued)

Below are the **past tense** forms of the verbs *be*, *do*, and *have*.

Be	Do	Have
I **was**, *he* **was**, *she* **was**, *it was*	*I* **did**, *he* **did**, *she* **did**, *it* **did**	*I* **had**, *he* **had**, *she* **had**, *it* **had**
we **were**, *you* **were**, *they* **were**	*we* **did**, *you* **did**, *they* **did**	*we* **had**, *you* **had**, *they* **had**

4. Circle the correct **past tense** form of the verb in brackets.

   a) He (was were) very excited about going to the zoo.

   b) She (has had) a cold last week, but she feels better now.

   c) We (do did) all of the chores on our list.

   d) It (had has) three buttons, but one button fell off.

   e) You (was were) right, and I (was were) wrong.

   f) They (has had) three cats, but they gave one to us.

5. Choose the correct verb (**be**, **do**, or **have**). Then write the correct **past tense** form of the verb.

   a) It _____ a sunny day when we went hiking last week.

   b) They _____ all the work in a very short time.

   c) He _____ several coins in the pocket of his jeans.

   d) They _____ on the top shelf the last time I looked.

   e) We _____ lots of fun playing tag with the other children.

   f) You _____ very helpful to me when I had a broken arm.

More Practice with *Be*, *Do*, and *Have*

Review the **present tense** and **past tense** forms of the verbs *be*, *do*, and *have*.

Present Tense

	Be	Do	Have
I	*am*	*do*	*have*
he, she, it	*is*	*does*	*has*
we, you, they	*are*	*do*	*have*

Past Tense

	Be	Do	Have
I, he, she, it	*was*	*did*	*had*
we, you, they	*were*	*did*	*had*

1. Look at the **verb** in bold. Is it in the **present tense** or **past tense**? Circle your answer, then **check** the charts above to see if your answer is correct.

a) We **were** all excited about going to the circus.   **present past**

b) I wonder if she **is** still at home.   **present past**

c) They **had** lots of fun at the amusement park.   **present past**

d) He **did** the grocery shopping this morning.   **present past**

e) It **has** a power button to turn the television on or off.   **present past**

f) You **are** always on time for basketball practice.   **present past**

g) She **was** interested in learning more about whales.   **present past**

h) We **do** the dishes as soon as we have finished eating.   **present past**

i) My best friend **does** lots of favours for me.   **present past**

More Practice with *Be*, *Do*, and *Have* (continued)

2. Read each sentence and decide whether it needs a **present tense** or **past tense** verb. Then write the **correct form** of the verb in brackets.

a) Last year, she _____ in Grade 2. (be)

b) Now you _____ five minutes left to finish the quiz. (have)

c) He _____ the laundry last Wednesday. (do)

d) We _____ very busy all day yesterday. (be)

e) I _____ happy because my grandparents are visiting. (be)

f) You still _____ lots of time to do your homework now. (have)

g) They _____ two word search puzzles last night. (do)

3. Read each sentence and decide whether it needs a **present tense verb** or a **past tense verb**. Then choose the correct verb (*be*, *do*, or *have*) and write the **correct form** of the verb.

a) Last month, it _____ cloudy almost every day.

b) She _____ some stretches to warm up before the race started.

c) I _____ a cut on my finger, but it will heal soon.

d) It is almost lunchtime, so we _____ hungry.

e) They _____ no trouble falling asleep last night.

f) He _____ a jigsaw puzzle, then he cleaned his room.

g) You _____ a better goalie now than you were last year.

h) We _____ our homework before we watched the movie.

i) He used to have one cat, but now he _____ two.

Linking Verbs

A **linking verb** is a verb that does **not** show **action**.
The verb *be* is a linking verb.

Remember that the verb *be* has different forms.
The **present tense** forms of *be* are *am*, *is*, and *are*.
The **past tense** forms of *be* are *was* and *were*.

Compare the **verbs** in the example sentences below.

*Example: Shauna **kicks** the ball.*
Kicks is an action, so **kicks** is an action verb.

*Example: The twins **are** eight years old.*
Are is **not** an action, so **are** is **not** an action verb. **Are** is a **linking verb**. (Remember that **are** is a present tense form of the verb **be**.)

A **linking verb** connects the **subject** of the sentence (the person or thing the sentence is about) to a **noun** or an **adjective**. Look at the examples below.

*Example: This <u>girl</u> **is** my <u>cousin</u>.*
The linking verb **is** connects the **subject** of the sentence (*girl*) to a **noun** (*cousin*).

*Example: The <u>children</u> **were** <u>hungry</u>.*
The linking verb **were** connects the **subject** of the sentence (*children*) to an **adjective** (*hungry*).

*Example: <u>Mr. Wilson</u> **was** a <u>teacher</u>.*
The linking verb **was** connects the **subject** of the sentence (*Mr. Wilson*) to a **noun** (*teacher*).

*Example: <u>We</u> **are** <u>excited</u>.*
The linking verb **are** connects the **subject** of the sentence (*We*) to an **adjective** (*excited*).

Canadian Grammar Practice 3 © Chalkboard Publishing

Linking Verbs (continued)

1. In the sentences below, the **verbs** are in bold. Circle all the **linking** verbs. Underline all the **action** verbs.

   a) The windows **were** dirty.

   b) Lisa **ran** all the way home.

   c) This joke **is** funny.

   d) These flowers **are** colourful.

   e) The glass **fell** off the table.

   f) I **am** tired today.

2. Find the **verbs** in the sentences below. Circle all the **linking** verbs. Underline all the **action** verbs.

   a) Mr. Yang painted a beautiful picture. He is an artist.

   b) These grapes are delicious. Let us eat some more.

   c) All the flowers were lovely. I picked a red flower for Mom.

   d) I am a carpenter. I build cupboards and shelves.

   e) My little puppy is cute. It was a gift from my parents.

   f) Angela slipped on some ice. She fell on the sidewalk.

   g) The movies were funny. We laughed a lot!

   h) These pictures are nice. The children drew them.

   i) We swam in the lake. The water was very cold!

   j) I am excited. Today is my birthday!

Spelling Present Tense Verbs

For most **present tense** verbs, add **s** if **he**, **she**, or **it** does the action.
Watch out for verbs that need tricky spelling changes!
For verbs that end in a **consonant + y**, change the **y** to **i** and add **es**.

Examples: *I study – she studies*   *they carry – he carries*

For verbs that end with **s**, **x**, **ch**, or **sh**, add **es**.

Examples: *I kiss – she kisses*   *I fix – he fixes*
              they pinch – it pinches   *you wish – he wishes*

1. In the blank, write the correct **present tense** of the verb in brackets.

a) She _____ the words from the board. (copy)

b) The little boy _____ because he is scared. (cry)

c) Max _____ carrots and onions. (buy)

d) The kite _____ in the wind. (fly)

e) The raccoon _____ to climb over the fence. (try)

2. In the blank, write the correct **present tense** of the verb in brackets.

a) My brother _____ his mosquito bite. (scratch)

b) Alice _____ the button on the elevator. (push)

c) Marcus _____ the stack of papers. (pass)

d) She _____ the flour and fruit together. (mix)

e) The bucket _____ the drops of water. (catch)

Past Tense Verbs

Past tense verbs tell what happened in the past. Look at these examples:

Verb	Present Tense	Past Tense
talk	Today, I talk.	Yesterday, I talked.
	Today, she talks.	Yesterday, she talked.

For many verbs, add **ed** to the verb to make the past tense.
If the verb already ends with **e**, just add **d**.

1. Write the **past tense** of the verbs below. Add **ed** or **d** to make the past tense.

   a) invent _____

   b) cough _____

   c) share _____

   d) work _____

   e) borrow _____

   f) escape _____

   g) agree _____

   h) explode _____

2. Complete each sentence. Write the **past tense** of the verb in brackets to show that the action happened in the past.

   a) The dog _____ the squirrel. (chase)

   b) Leon _____ his food slowly. (chew)

   c) Kelly _____ the sink with water. (fill)

3. Is the verb in each sentence **present tense** or **past tense**? Write **present** or **past** beside each sentence.

   a) Mom glued the pieces back together. _____

   b) We race along the path through the park. _____

   c) Jonathan rinses the shampoo out of his hair. _____

Spelling Past Tense Verbs

For many verbs that end with **consonant + vowel + consonant**, double the final consonant before adding *ed*.

Examples: *hop – hopped*   *clap – clapped*   *zip – zipped*

For most verbs that end with a **consonant + y**, change the *y* to an *i* and add *ed*.

Examples: *study – studied*   *marry – married*

1. Write the **past tense** of the verb in brackets. For each verb, double the final consonant before adding *ed*.

   a) Jeremy _____ on a rock. (trip)

   b) The car _____ at the red light. (stop)

   c) Dad made the soup, and I _____ it. (stir)

   d) Ella _____ paint on the floor. (drip)

   e) Richard _____ over the puddle. (step)

2. Write the **past tense** of the verb in brackets.

   a) The baby _____ when he dropped his rattle. (cry)

   b) The movers _____ the heavy boxes. (carry)

   c) They _____ to the party. (hurry)

   d) Eva _____ about her lost dog. (worry)

Tricky Past Tense Verbs

The **past tense** of some verbs does not end with **ed**. Watch out for these tricky verbs when you use the past tense!

Present Tense	Past Tense
come, comes	came
drive, drives	drove
eat, eats	ate
fall, falls	fell

Present Tense	Past Tense
get, gets	got
give, gives	gave
have, has	had
say, says	said

1. Write the **past tense** of the verb in brackets.

   a) Lina _____ a cold last week. (have)

   b) Yesterday, Jacob _____ he wanted to visit us. (say)

   c) Who _____ all the snacks? (eat)

   d) The principal _____ to our classroom. (come)

2. Rewrite each sentence. Change the **past tense verb** to **present tense**.

   a) We drove to the grocery store.

   _____

   b) The squirrel ate all the nuts.

   _____

   c) I had two pencils in my desk.

   _____

   d) Carly came to my house every week.

   _____

Tricky Past Tense Verbs (continued)

Watch out for these tricky verbs when you use the **past tense**!

Present Tense	Past Tense
buy, buys	brought
draw, draws	drove
drink, drinks	drank
find, finds	found

Present Tense	Past Tense
know, knows	knew
go, goes	went
take, takes	took
think, thinks	thought

3. Write the **past tense** of the verb in brackets.

a) We _____ along the path through the forest. (go)

b) Brendan _____ a glass of milk with his sandwich. (drink)

c) I _____ my answer was correct. (think)

d) Emily _____ some pretty flowers at the market. (buy)

4. Rewrite each sentence. Change the **past tense verb** to **present tense**.

a) We drank juice with our breakfast.

_____

b) He bought a new toy for his grandson.

_____

c) Anna found lots of seashells at the beach.

_____

d) I thought about my best friend.

_____

Canadian Grammar Practice 3 © Chalkboard Publishing

Future Tense Verbs

Future tense verbs tell about things that will happen in the future.
To make future tense verbs, use the helping verb *will*.

One Person or Thing	More Than One Person or Thing
I will walk	We will walk
You will walk	You will walk
He/She/It will walk	They will walk

1. Complete each sentence. Write the **future tense** of the verb in brackets to show that the action will happen in the future.

a) Tomorrow, they _____ a horse. (ride)

b) Next week, Sandy _____ in the pool. (swim)

c) This morning, the sun _____. (shine)

d) In ten minutes, Dad _____ me home. (drive)

2. Rewrite each sentence. Change the **past tense** verb to a **future tense** verb.

a) Timothy planted a tree in the backyard.

_____

b) Carlos and Mary talked about the movie.

_____

c) People laughed at all my silly jokes.

_____

Helping Verbs: Present and Future Tenses

A **main verb** tells what someone or something is or does. Look at the example below.

Example: Mr. Silver <u>cooks</u> dinner.

A **helping verb** works with a **main verb** to show action. Use the helping verbs *is*, *am*, and *are* to tell about things that are happening **now**.

In the sentences below, the **main verb** is underlined, and the **helping verb** is in bold. All the sentences tell about an action that is happening **now**.

*Examples: Mr. Jenkins **is** <u>cooking</u> dinner.*
*I **am** <u>cooking</u> dinner.*
*My parents **are** <u>cooking</u> dinner.*

Use the helping verbs *is*, *am*, and *are* with **main verbs** that end with *ing*.

1. Circle the correct **helping verb** in brackets to tell about an action that is happening now. Underline the **main verb** in each sentence.

   a) Paula (is am are) looking for her sunglasses.

   b) The wind (is am are) blowing leaves off the trees.

   c) I (is am are) brushing my teeth.

   d) The dogs (is am are) chasing the cat.

   e) My father (is am are) cutting the grass with the new lawnmower.

   f) Now I (is am are) working on my science project.

   g) We (is am are) pulling weeds from the garden.

   h) My neighbours (is am are) washing their windows.

Canadian Grammar Practice 3 © Chalkboard Publishing

Helping Verbs: Present and Future Tenses (continued)

Use the **helping verb *will*** to tell about things that will happen in the **future**. Look at the examples below.

*Examples: Tony **will** <u>clean</u> his room in a few minutes.*
*Samantha **will** <u>arrive</u> tomorrow afternoon.*

Notice that when you use ***will*** before a **main verb**, the main verb does **not** end with ***ing***.

2. Rewrite each sentence to make the action happen in the **future**. Use the helping verb ***will***. Look at the example below.

Examples: The garbage truck is coming.
The garbage truck will come.

a) The children are planting tulips.

_____

b) We hang the pictures on the wall.

_____

c) I am singing my favourite song.

_____

d) The birds are building a nest in the tree.

_____

e) They ask the librarian some questions.

_____

Helping Verbs: Past Tense

A **helping verb** works with a **main verb** to show an action. Use the helping verbs **has**, **had**, and **have** to tell about things that have **already happened**. Look at the examples below. The **main verb** is underlined, and the **helping verb** is in bold.

*Examples: The rain **has** <u>stopped</u>.*
*My neighbour **had** <u>painted</u> her house.*
*The students **have** <u>made</u> signs for the bake sale.*

1. Circle the correct **helping verb** in brackets to tell about an action that has already happened. Underline the **main verb** in each sentence.

a) My grandmother (has have) walked to the grocery store.

b) My dog (have had) chewed a hole in my sock.

c) These plants (have has) grown taller since last week.

d) Three apples (has have) dropped from the apple tree.

e) The paint on the picnic table (have has) dried quickly.

f) The car (had have) stopped at the red light.

g) The children (have has) wrapped all the gifts.

h) I (has have) played with the cat earlier that morning.

i) They (have has) built a doghouse for their dog.

j) Julie (have has) invited me to the party.

k) All the snow (had have) melted during the warm weather.

Helping Verbs: Past Tense (continued)

Use the **helping verbs** *was* and *were* to tell about things that have **already happened**. Look at the examples below. The **main verb** is underlined, and the **helping verb** is in bold.

*Examples: My brother **was** <u>helping</u> Mom clean up.*
*The flags **were** <u>flapping</u> in the wind.*

Notice that *was* and *were* are used with **main verbs** that end with *ing*.

2. Circle the correct **helping verb** in brackets to tell about an action that has already happened.

   a) The telephone (was   were) ringing when I got home.

   b) The firefighters (was   were) putting out a fire.

   c) Some women (was   were) watching their children in the park.

   d) He (was   were) looking at the lightning in the sky.

   e) Aunt Joan (was   were) raking leaves from her lawn.

   f) My new shoes (was   were) hurting my feet.

3. Circle the correct **main verb** to use with the **helping verb** in each sentence.

   a) Shauna has (walks   walked   walking) to the library and back.

   b) Last night, the crickets were (chirp   chirping   chirped).

   c) He was (climbs   climbing   climbed) up the oak tree.

   d) The cooks were (stir   stirring   stirred) large pots of soup.

   e) I was (collect   collecting   collected) coins from many different countries.

Subject–Verb Agreement

The **subject** of a **verb** is the person, people, thing, or things doing the action.
In the examples below, the **subject** of the verb is in bold, and the **verb** is underlined.

*Examples: The **children** <u>laugh</u> at the joke.*
*The **child** <u>laughs</u> at the joke*

Notice that in the second sentence above, an **s** is added to the verb **laugh**. Sometimes, you need to change the spelling of a **present tense verb** to make the correct form to use with the **subject**. Here are two more examples:

*Examples: The **men** <u>wash</u> the dog.*
*The **man** <u>washes</u> the dog.*

Notice that sometimes you need to add **es** to a **present tense verb** to make the correct form of the verb for the **subject**.

When the verb is in the **correct form** for the **subject**, we say that the subject and verb "**agree**."

1. Write the correct form of the **verb** in brackets. Make sure the subject and the verb **agree**.

a) The horse _____ across the field. (run)

b) The moon _____ at night. (glows)

c) The boats _____ across the lake. (sails)

d) These weeds _____ quickly! (grow)

e) Janelle _____ a mosquito bite. (scratch)

f) The women _____ for cooler weather. (run)

g) The cat _____ the mouse across the lawn. (follow)

h) The twins _____ out their candles. (blows)

Subject–Verb Agreement (continued)

2. Circle the correct **present tense** form of the verb to make the subject and verb **agree**.

a) My sister always (study studies) very hard.

b) Snow (fall falls) all day long.

c) The workers (unload unloads) lots of boxes from the truck.

d) Janice (brush brushes) her teeth after every meal.

e) The squirrels (bury buries) acorns in our lawn.

f) The police officers (look looks) for the thieves.

3. Write the correct **present tense** form of the verb in brackets to make the subject and verb **agree**.

a) The doctor _____ to the sick patient. (rush)

b) Carlos _____ that show every week. (watch)

c) People _____ silly things sometimes. (say)

d) The boy _____ across the puddle. (jump)

e) The children _____ the national anthem. (sing)

f) Slowly, the caterpillar _____ across the floor. (creep)

g) After dinner, my brother often _____ for a walk. (go)

h) My friends sometimes _____ their bikes in the park. (ride)

i) The angry cat _____ at the raccoon. (hiss)

Pronoun–Verb Agreement

The **subject** of a **verb** is the person, people, thing, or things doing the action. In the examples below, the **subject** of the verb is in bold, and the **verb** is underlined.

*Examples: **Crickets** <u>chirp</u> in the long grass.*
*The **worker** <u>climbs</u> up the tall ladder.*

Sometimes, the **subject** of a verb is a **pronoun**. In the examples below, the **pronoun** that is the **subject** of the verb is in bold, and the **verb** is underlined.

*Examples: **He** <u>takes</u> the money off the table.*
***They** <u>give</u> the children some oranges.*

When the verb is in the **correct form** for the **subject**, we say that the subject and verb "agree."

The **subject** and **verb** always need to **agree**, even when the subject is a **pronoun**. Remember:
• For most **present tense action verbs**, add *s* or *es* if the subject is **he**, **she**, or **it**.
• **Do not** add *s* or *es* if the subject is **I, you, we,** or **they**.

---

1. Write the correct form of the **verb** in brackets. Make sure the subject and the verb **agree**.

a) It _____ the colour of your eyes. (match)

b) We _____ lightning in the cloudy sky. (see)

c) She _____ the hole in the roof. (fix)

d) Suddenly, they _____ all the way home. (runs)

e) I _____ all the marbles in the bag. (count)

f) He _____ the dog's toy under the couch. (find)

g) You _____ Jessie your colour pencils. (lend)

Canadian Grammar Practice 3 © Chalkboard Publishing

Pronoun–Verb Agreement (continued)

2. Write the correct **present tense** form of the **verb** in brackets to make the **subject** and **verb agree**.

a) He _____ the baby on the cheek. (kiss)

b) Sometimes, you _____ your shoelaces too tightly. (tie)

c) Usually, it _____ a loud noise when it falls over. (make)

d) She _____ a muffin for herself and one for her brother. (take)

e) He _____ the bump on his forehead. (touch)

f) We _____ a new person has joined our team. (notice)

g) I carefully _____ each bite of food. (chew)

h) She _____ the goal on her last shot at the net. (miss)

3. Circle the correct **present tense** form of the verb in brackets to make the **pronoun subject** and the **verb agree**. Then see if you can answer the riddle.

a) It (keep keeps) you warm in bed on chilly nights. What is it? _____

b) They (make makes) a flashlight's bulb light up. What are they? _____

c) It (buzz buzzes) to wake you up in the morning. What is it? _____

d) They (help helps) some people see better. What are they? _____

e) It (go goes) around your waist. What is it? _____

f) They (come comes) to put out a fire. What are they? _____

Verbs Review Quiz 1

1. Circle all the **verbs** in each sentence.

    a) My fingernails grow longer and longer until I cut them.

    b) Our team cheers whenever one of our players hits a home run.

    c) We climb the tree and pick some apples.

    d) I erased the incorrect answer and wrote the correct one.

2. Circle all the **verbs** in each list.

    a) make   stapler   tell   takes   sheet   beautiful

    b) playful   happy   find   sad   ask   job   sees

    c) hard   write   worst   listen   toaster   bring

3. Write the correct **present tense** form of the verb in brackets. (The present tense tells about actions that are happening **now**.)

    a) Dad _____ the cooking in my family. (do)

    b) She _____ the leaky tap. (fix)

    c) You _____ the ball and throw it to Noah. (catch)

    d) It _____ up in the sky and out into space. (fly)

    e) Sheila _____ new winter boots at the store. (buy)

    f) The shot _____ the goal. (miss)

    g) I _____ the captain of my hockey team. (be)

    Canadian Grammar Practice 3 © Chalkboard Publishing

Verbs Review Quiz 1 (continued)

4. Write the correct **past tense** form of the verb in brackets. (The past tense tells about actions that have **already happened**.)

a) The man _____ all the way home in the winter storm. (walk)

b) The audience _____ loudly when the play was over. (clap)

c) Nick _____ sick all last week. (be)

d) Some workers _____ long boards into the new house. (carry)

e) We _____ a jigsaw puzzle before we went to bed. (finish)

f) The truck _____ slowly down the road. (drive)

g) They _____ milk, cheese, and vegetables. (buy)

h) Nobody _____ the answer to my question. (know)

i) The children _____ excited about going to the circus. (be)

5. Write the correct **future tense** form of the verb in brackets. (The future tense tells about actions that will happen **in the future**.) Remember to use a **helping verb**.

a) Tomorrow, I _____ you to tell you what time to come. (call)

b) Maria _____ us her story next. (read)

c) My grandparents _____ us next week. (visit)

d) You _____ even taller next year. (grow)

e) We _____ a cake for his birthday. (make)

Verbs Review Quiz 2

1. Circle the **linking** verbs and underline the **action** verbs.

   a) The weather was cold. I found my warm jacket.

   b) I read comic books. They are exciting!

   c) You were sad, so I told you a funny joke.

   d) The television show was good, but the commercials were boring.

2. Circle each **helping verb** and underline each **main verb**.

   a) The rain is making us wet!

   b) The cars were honking at us.

   c) I am running faster than the other people in the race.

   d) You are singing a very pretty song.

3. Write the correct form of the **verb** in brackets. Make sure the subject and the verb **agree**.

   a) The squirrels _____ up the elm tree. (climbs)

   b) An elephant _____ its long trunk in different ways. (uses)

   c) He _____ green eyes and black hair. (have)

   d) You _____ a little bit taller than me. (is)

   e) They _____ a quarter and two dimes on the sidewalk. (find)

   f) She _____ her teeth after each meal. (brush)

 Canadian Grammar Practice 3 © Chalkboard Publishing

Verbs Review Quiz 2 (continued)

4. Write the correct **present tense** form of the **helping verb** in brackets.

a) The waves _____ crashing on the shore. (be)

b) He _____ helping Mom paint the kitchen. (be)

c) I _____ sweeping up the crumbs on the floor. (be)

d) We _____ hoping the sun will come out soon. (be)

5. Rewrite each sentence to show the action happening in the **future**.

a) The hungry lions hunt for food.

_____

b) I walk to the grocery store.

_____

6. Circle the correct **helping verb** in brackets to tell about an action that has **already happened**.

a) The loud thunder (was   were   is) scaring the little children.

b) I (had   has) written my name at the top of the quiz.

c) The snowflakes (are   were   was) melting on my face.

d) She (have   has) promised to help me.

e) Our neighbours (have   has) invited us to a barbecue.

f) They (is   was   were) whispering secrets to each other.

Some Adverbs Describe How

An **adverb** describes a verb. An adverb can describe **how, when**, **where**, or **how often** an action happens.

On this page, you will work with adverbs that describe **how** an action happens.

Example: Tara quickly tied her shoes.

The adverb *quickly* describes **how** Tara tied her shoes.

In the example above, the adverb comes **before** the verb it describes.
An adverb can also come **after** the verb it describes.

Examples: The woman spoke <u>softly</u>.   Eric ran up the steps <u>quickly</u>.

1. Underline the **adverb** that tells **how** an action happens.

   a) Fred slowly walked home.

   b) She quietly left the room.

   c) Carmella loudly shouted the answer.

   d) The boys carefully washed the glasses.

   e) The students correctly answered all of the questions.

   f) The father gently held his baby daughter.

2. Underline the **adverb** that tells **how** an action happens.

   a) The ballerina danced gracefully across the stage.

   b) The painters hummed happily as they worked.

   c) Leon answered the questions honestly.

   d) The grandmother smiled sweetly at her grandson.

   e) Susan held the baseball bat tightly.

   f) The thief tiptoed silently from the room.

Some Adverbs Describe When

An **adverb** describes a verb. An adverb can describe **how, when**, **where,** or **how often** an action happens.

On this page, you will work with **adverbs** that describe **when** an action happens.

Example: Cathy will visit us <u>tomorrow</u>.

The adverb *tomorrow* describes **when** Cathy will visit.

1. Underline only the adverbs that tell **when** an action happens.

   a) The children played noisily in the park this afternoon.

   b) Maggie will read her story next.

   c) Tomorrow, Alfredo will make a special dinner.

   d) Please close the window now.

   e) The rain will stop soon.

   f) The girls quickly cleaned up the mess at lunchtime.

   g) Yesterday, the dentist checked my teeth.

   h) Next, I will show you an amazing magic trick.

   i) The fire alarm rang, so Fernando left the building immediately.

2. Read each sentence and underline the **adverb.** Then complete the next sentence.

   a) Later, we will sing a song.

      The adverb _____ tells **when** the action _____ happens.

   b) Walt will swim next.

      The adverb _____ tells **when** the action _____ happens.

   c) Soon my friend will arrive.

      The adverb _____ tells **when** the action _____ happens.

Some Adverbs Describe Where

An **adverb** describes a verb. An adverb can describe **how, when, where,** or **how often** an action happens.

On this page, you will work with **adverbs** that describe **where** an action happens.

Example: Eddie and Tyler look <u>outside</u>.

The adverb *outside* describes **where** Eddie and Tyler look.

Some **adverbs** describe **where** something happens, but they **do not** describe the **exact place**.

Example: Abdul hid his book <u>somewhere</u>.

The adverb *somewhere* describes **where** Abdul hid his book.

1. Read the sentence and underline the **adverb**. Then complete the next sentence.

   a) I hang the picture here.

   The adverb _____ tells **where** the action _____ happens.

   b) Penny plays inside on rainy days.

   The adverb _____ tells **where** the action _____ happens.

   c) My brother found his book downstairs.

   The adverb _____ tells **where** the action _____ happens.

   d) They put the flowers there.

   The adverb _____ tells **where** the action _____ happens.

2. Underline the adverb that tells **where** an action happens.

   a) I searched everywhere for my umbrella.

   b) The frightened bird flew away.

   c) A lion roared nearby.

   d) You can put your coats anywhere.

   e) They hid the treasure somewhere.

Canadian Grammar Practice 3 © Chalkboard Publishing

Some Adverbs Describe How Often

An **adverb** describes a verb. An adverb can describe **how, when**, **where**, or **how often** an action happens.

On this page, you will work with **adverbs** that describe **how often** an action happens.

Example: They <u>sometimes</u> go camping in August.

The adverb **sometimes** describes **how often** they go camping in August.

Learn these **adverbs** that describe **how often** an action happens.

constantly (all the time)   **occasionally** (once in a while)
frequently (very often)   **seldom** (not very often)
usually (most of the time)   **rarely** (almost never)

1. Underline the adverb that tells **how often** an action happens.

   a) My neighbour always waves at me.

   b) Molly rang the doorbell twice.

   c) Mr. Cortez often hums his favourite song.

   d) My baby sister never cries.

   e) I flew on an airplane once.

2. In the **second** sentence, write one of the **adverbs** from the list above. Choose an adverb that **means the same** as the underlined words.

   a) Sam eats yogurt <u>very often</u>.   Sam _____ eats yogurt.

   b) The baby cries <u>all the time</u>.   The baby cries _____.

   c) I <u>almost never</u> catch a cold.   I _____ catch a cold.

   d) It rains <u>most of the time</u>.   It _____ rains.

   e) He dreams <u>not very often</u>.   He _____ dreams.

   f) You sneeze <u>once in a while</u>.   You sneeze _____.

Adverbs Review Quiz

1. The **adverbs** in the sentences below describe **how** an action happens. Circle the adverbs.

   a) The salesperson cheerfully asked if I needed any help.

   b) The man yelled angrily at the raccoons in his garden.

   c) This student has correctly answered all the questions.

   d) Carol gently put the crying baby in the crib.

   e) Ivan politely asked if he could join our game of hide-and-seek.

   f) The children had safely crossed the street when the light turned red.

   g) If you want to tell me a secret, whisper it quietly in my ear.

2. The **adverbs** in the sentences below describe **when** an action happens. Circle the adverbs.

   a) It snowed yesterday, and we made snowmen in the park.

   b) Mom is busy, but she will call you later.

   c) I am sure the bus will come soon.

   d) If the children are hungry, we can eat lunch now.

   e) Leon is happy that the sun is shining today.

   f) Rachel is taking her turn, and Roger will go next.

   g) Mr. and Mrs. Gallo will fly to France tomorrow.

   h) Dad left for work late.

Adverbs Review Quiz (continued)

3. The **adverbs** in the sentences below describe **where** an action happens. Circle the adverbs.

a) Let us wait here and see if the rain stops.

b) Mom went downstairs to answer the door.

c) I think I left my keys somewhere in the living room.

d) The women sat outside to enjoy the sunshine.

4. The **adverbs** in the sentences below describe **how often** an action happens. Circle the adverbs.

a) Mrs. Kirby always feeds her cat in the morning.

b) Joel often wins when I play checkers with him.

c) I never cross the street before I look both ways.

d) She called them twice, but no one answered the phone.

5. Circle the correct word to tell what the bold **adverb** describes.

a) My sister touched me **lightly** on the shoulder.
   The adverb *lightly* describes (how when where how often).

b) Water the plant **weekly,** or the soil will dry out.
   The adverb *weekly* describes (how when where how often).

c) Melissa is not hungry, so she will eat **later**.
   The adverb *later* describes (how when where how often).

d) We stayed **inside** because the day was so cold.
   The adverb *inside* describes (how when where how often).

Complete Subjects

There are two parts to a sentence. These parts are called the **complete subject** and the **complete predicate**. We will talk about complete predicates in another lesson.

The **complete subject** contains all the words that tell **who or what** the sentence is about. In the examples below, the complete subject is in bold.

*Example: **The tiny black kitten** snuggled beside its mother.*

This sentence is about a kitten. The complete subject contains **all** the words that tell about the kitten.

*Example: **The bright lightning** lit up the night sky.*

This sentence is about lightening. The complete subject contains **all** the words that tell about the lightening.

In each sentence, underline all the words in the **complete subject**.

a) The sly fox snuck into the hen house.

b) Several silly clowns were lined up for the parade.

c) Many different types of seashells were found onshore.

d) The lights of the city twinkled down below.

e) A large black bear wandered through our campsite.

f) My friend Jessica played an apple tree in our school play.

g) Many children in my class wear glasses.

h) The people of the town held a strawberry festival.

i) Fire trucks and firefighters rushed to put out the fire.

Complete Predicates

In a previous lesson, we talked about complete subject of a sentence, which tells who or what the sentence is about. Now we will talk about the rest of the sentence: The **complete predicate**.

The **complete predicate** includes the **verb** and **all** the words that tell about what happened in the sentence. In the examples below, the complete predicate is underlined.

Example: The forest fire <u>crept closer to the town</u>.

The verb in this sentence is *crept*. The other underlined words help to tell about what happened in the sentence.

Example: The ocean waves <u>washed the children's sand castle away</u>.

The verb in this sentence is *washed*. The other underlined words help to tell about what happened in the sentence.

Every word in a sentence will be part the complete subject **or** part of the complete predicate. In the examples below, the complete subject is in bold, and the complete predicate is underlined.

Examples: **The happy puppies** <u>chased a ball in our backyard</u>.
Hens with red feathers <u>lay brown eggs.</u>.

In each sentence, underline all the words in the **complete predicate**.

a) A little green duck swims in our pool every day.

b) Little red beetles ate all my mother's lilies.

c) Seven brown puppies tumbled out of the box.

d) My sister and I made peanut butter sandwiches.

e) Some people read newspapers only on weekends.

f) My parents painted my bedroom mint green today.

g) This week's math homework contains multiplication problems.

h) The striped rubber ball rolled all the way down the hill.

What Comes at the End of a Sentence?

Put a **period** at the end of a **telling sentence**.

Example: We are going to the park.

Put a **question mark** at the end of a **question sentence**.

Example: Did you bring your umbrella?

Put an **exclamation mark** at the end of a sentence that shows a **strong feeling**. Anger, happiness, and excitement are examples of strong feelings.

Examples: You hurt me!   This is fun!   I can't wait!

Put a **period** or an **exclamation mark** at the end of a **command** sentence.

A **command** sentence tells someone to do something.

Examples: Hang your coat up.   Watch out!

---

1. Write the correct punctuation mark at the end of each sentence.

   a) Would you like a slice of pizza____

   b) Stop making so much noise____

   c) Hooray, we are going to the zoo____

   d) Are you going to the library____

   e) The girls are watching the parade____

   f) Be careful____

   g) What is your favourite season of the year____

What Comes at the End of a Sentence? (continued)

2. Write two examples of each kind of sentence. Be sure to include the correct punctuation at the end of each sentence.

a) Telling sentence:

_____

_____

_____

b) Asking sentence:

_____

_____

_____

c) Sentence that shows strong feeling:

_____

_____

_____

d) Command sentence:

_____

_____

One Sentence or Two?

A short sentence usually tells **one idea**.

Examples: My mother lost her ring. (one idea)

I found it in the bathroom. (one idea)

Be careful when you write sentences. Check to see if you need to turn one sentence into two sentences.

*Example: This is **not** correct: I saw a puppy it was lost.*

*This is **correct**: I saw a puppy. It was lost.*

The sentences below are **not** correct. Correct each sentence by writing it as **two sentences**.

a) I like Lisa she is my friend.

_____

b) Pak likes to run he runs fast.

_____

c) It was raining I got wet.

_____

d) Dad read a story it was funny.

_____

e) The telephone rang it woke me up.

_____

Remember to check your writing. Did you start each sentence with a capital letter?

Canadian Grammar Practice 3 © Chalkboard Publishing

Joining Sentences with *And* or *But*

You can use **and** to join together two short sentences.

Example: John bought crayons. He drew pictures.
John bought crayons, and he drew pictures.

You can also use **but** to join together short sentences. Use **but** when the idea in the **second** sentence **goes against** the idea in the **first** sentence.

Example: Donna wants to stay up late. Her mom said no.
Donna wants to stay up late, but her mom said no.

1. Read the two sentences. Then use **and** or **but** to **join together** the two sentences. Write the **best word** to join the sentences.

   a) Carlos wanted to swim. He forgot his bathing suit.
      Carlos wanted to swim, _____ he forgot his bathing suit.

   b) She washes the dishes. I dry them
      She washes the dishes, _____ I dry them.

   c) Norma was not hungry. She ate a salad.
      Norma was not hungry, _____ she ate a salad.

   d) I like the zoo. We are going there tomorrow.
      I like the zoo, _____ we are going there tomorrow.

2. Each sentence below was made by joining together two short sentences. Complete each sentence by writing the joining word **and** or **but**. Put a comma **before** the joining word.

   a) The sun is shining _____ it is a nice day.

   b) Hans watered the plant _____ it died.

   c) I wore a warm coat _____ I was still cold.

   d) Jana likes reading _____ she reads often.

   e) Dad found his glasses _____ he lost them again.

Joining Sentences with *Or* or *So*

You can use *or* to join together two short sentences. Use *or* when each sentence tells about two **different** actions, and only **one** action will happen.

Example: We can eat spaghetti for dinner tonight. We can eat chicken.
We can eat spaghetti for dinner tonight, or we can eat chicken.

You can use *so* to join together two short sentences. Use *so* when the idea in the **second** sentence happens **because of** the idea in the **first** sentence.

Example: It was raining. I took my umbrella.
It was raining, so I took my umbrella.

1. Write *or* or *so* to join together the sentences.

   a) We could walk to the park. We could ride our bikes there.

      We could walk to the park, _____ we could ride our bikes there.

   b) Tina might arrive on time. She might be late.

      Tina might arrive on time, _____ she might be late.

   c) My feet got wet. I dried them.

      My feet got wet, _____ I dried them.

   d) Raj was hungry. He ate a snack.

      Raj was hungry, _____ he ate a snack.

2. The sentences below were made by joining together two short sentences. Write the joining word *or* or *so*. Put a comma **before** the joining word.

   a) Her bike had a flat tire _____ she walked to school.

   b) I might keep this photo _____ I might give it to Stanley.

   c) Sandra might keep her hair long _____ she might get it cut short.

   d) Mika had dirty hands _____ he washed them.

 Canadian Grammar Practice 3 © Chalkboard Publishing

Sentences and Punctuation Review Quiz

1. Add the correct **punctuation mark** (period, exclamation mark, or question mark) at the end of the sentence. Then tell **what kind** of sentence it is (telling, question, strong feeling, or command).

   a) I love my kitten so much _____

   b) Tigers and zebras have stripes _____

   c) Speak louder so we can hear you _____

   d) Why did they leave so soon _____

   e) A rainbow appeared in the sky _____

   f) Is Hernando sick today _____

2. If the sentence should be **two** sentences, **rewrite** it as two sentences. If the sentence is **correct** as one sentence, write "Correct."

   a) Tina is funny she makes me laugh.

   _____

   b) The birds ate seeds at the feeder.

   _____

   c) The sun was shining it was a nice day.

   _____

   d) The dogs are barking they make lots of noise.

   _____

3. Use the correct joining word (*and* or *but*) to join the sentences. Remember to add a **comma** before the joining word.

   a) Alan plays piano. He practices every day.

   _____

   b) I was tired. I did not go to bed.

   _____

   c) Laura does not like grapes. She ate two anyway.

   _____

   d) The phone rang. Dad answered it.

   _____

   e) Wayne looks sick. He said he feels fine.

   _____

4. Circle the correct **joining word** in each sentence.

   a) The movie was boring, (or   so) we played a video game instead.

   b) It might snow tonight, (or   so) it might rain.

   c) We had read the newspapers, (or   so) we put them in the recycling bin.

   d) The computer was not working, (or   so) we asked Mom to fix it.

   e) We could make dinner, (or   so) we could eat at a restaurant.

What Is a Contraction?

A **contraction** is one word made from two words, with one or more of the letters **left out**. The letters that are left out are replaced by an **apostrophe** ('). Look at the examples below.

Two Words	Contraction
I am	I'm
you are	you're
he is	he's
she is	she's

Two Words	Contraction
it is	it's
that is	that's
we are	we're
they are	they're

1. In each sentence, write the **contraction** for the words in brackets.

a) They told me that _____ telling the truth. (they are)

b) _____ the youngest child in my family. (I am)

c) _____ moving to a new house next month. (We are)

d) Do you know that _____ my best friend? (you are)

e) _____ my birthday today. (It is)

f) Mom thinks _____ the funniest joke she ever heard. (that is)

2. Rewrite each sentence. Use **contractions** for the underlined words.

a) <u>She is</u> going to be upset if <u>he is</u> late.

_____

b) <u>I am</u> sure <u>that is</u> my notebook.

_____

More Contractions

A **contraction** is one word made from two words, with one or more of the letters **left out**. The letters that are left out are replaced by an **apostrophe** ('). Below are some examples of contractions made with the word *will*.

Two Words	Contraction
I will	*I'll*
you will	*you'll*
he will	*he'll*

Two Words	Contraction
she will	*she'll*
we will	*we'll*
they will	*they'll*

1. In each sentence, write the **contraction** for the words in brackets.

   a) _____ play baseball after school today. (We will)

   b) I hope _____ feel better tomorrow. (you will)

   c) I wonder if _____ help me find my mittens. (she will)

   d) _____ wait for you on the playground. (I will)

   e) _____ come to visit us next week. (They will)

   f) Do you think _____ win the race? (he will)

2. Rewrite the sentences below. Write each **contraction** as two words.

   a) I'll bring sandwiches, and you'll bring juice. We'll have a great picnic!

   _____

   _____

   _____

Abbreviations

An **abbreviation** is the **short form** of a word. An abbreviation ends with a **period**. The abbreviations in the sentence below are in bold.

Example: **Mrs.** *Lopez drove* **Mr.** *Rogers to the store.*

Mrs. is the abbreviation of **mistress**, and **Mr.** is the abbreviation of **mister**.

Below are two abbreviations you probably have seen before.

Example: **Dr.** *Rashad lives at 32 King* **St.**

Dr. is the abbreviation of **doctor**, and **St.** is the abbreviation of **street**.

Use **Dr.** only before someone's name. Look at the examples below.

Example: *I am going to see* **Dr.** *Johnson tomorrow.*

Dr. comes before the last name *Johnson*, so it is correct to use the abbreviation of **doctor**.

Example: *A* **doctor** *lives next door to us.*

In this sentence, **doctor** does **not** come before someone's name, so it would **not** be correct to use the abbreviation **Dr.**

Use **St.** only when it comes after the **name** of a street.

Example: *Carrie lives at 56 Forest* **St.**

St. comes after the name of a street, so it is correct to use the abbreviation.

Example: *I live on a* **street** *that is close to the hospital.*

Street does **not** come after the name of a street, so it would **not** be correct to use the abbreviation in this sentence.

Below are two more abbreviations you see in addresses. Like **St.**, use these abbreviations **only** when they come after a name.

Word	Abbreviation	Example
avenue	Ave.	*We are moving to 27 River* **Ave.**
road	Rd.	*The library is on Poplar* **Rd.**

Abbreviations (continued)

1. Circle the **correct choice** in brackets.

   a) I have an appointment to see (doctor Dr.) Harris tomorrow.

   b) We drove down a long and bumpy (road Rd.) to get there.

   c) Turn left when you get to Pine (street St.) and you'll see the hospital.

   d) They saw a long (avenue Ave.) with big trees on both sides.

   e) Is (doctor Dr.) Rosco the only (doctor Dr.) in the hospital right now?

   f) On Kingston (road Rd.), there are many new apartment buildings.

   g) Did you forget which (street St.) I live on?

   h) The school on Elm (avenue Ave.) has a large playground.

2. Rewrite the sentences below to show the proper use of **abbreviations**.

   a) Doctor Greyson went to school with Mrs Scott.

   _____

   b) Wilson ave. is near Westside Park.

   _____

   c) How close is Tower Rd to the office where mr. Patel works?

   _____

   d) Are there lots of trees on your st.?

   _____

Contractions and Abbreviations Review Quiz

1. In each sentence, write the **contraction** for the words in brackets.

   a) I am sure that _____ telling the truth. (he is)

   b) Do you think _____ going to be windy today? (it is)

   c) _____ finish painting this room tomorrow. (We will)

   d) It might rain, so _____ take my umbrella with me. (I will)

   e) _____ the funniest thing I have ever heard! (That is)

   f) When will you know if _____ be able to come? (you will)

   g) _____ still sleeping, so please be quiet. (They are)

2. In each sentence, write the **two words** for the contraction in brackets.

   a) We do not think _____ mind if we are a bit late. (she'll)

   b) I really like these pants _____ wearing today. (I'm)

   c) _____ going to go skating after lunch. (We're)

   d) There are two eggs in the nest, and _____ hatch very soon. (they'll)

   e) I think _____ going to win the game. (you're)

   f) _____ making cookies to sell at the bake sale. (She's)

   g) I am sure _____ help carry the boxes. (he'll)

   h) _____ be happy when they hear the good news. (They'll)

Contractions and Abbreviations Review Quiz (continued)

3. Write the **abbreviation** for the word in brackets.

   a) We saw _____ Tanaka at the grocery store. (Doctor)

   b) I saw _____ Gordon jogging in the park. (Mister)

   c) They rode their bikes down the hill on Lakeside _____ (Avenue).

   d) My aunt lived on Forest _____ before she moved. (Road)

4. Rewrite each sentence to correct any errors. Check to see if **abbreviations** and **contractions** are used correctly.

   a) Your going to be taller than you're father.

   _____

   b) Mrs Henderson thinks thats a wonderful idea.

   _____

   c) Hes certain that Alfonso lives on this St.

   _____

   d) Their walking they're dog along Wilson Rd.

   _____

   e) Western Ave is closed because its flooded.

   _____

Using *To, Too,* or *Two*

The word *to* can be used in different ways.

You can use *to* before a verb.
Example: I like to swim.

To can show where someone or something is going.
Examples: I am walking to school.   She is giving the book to Carlos.

The word *too* can be used in different ways.

Too can mean *also*.
Example: Bob sings, and Anna sings, too.

Too can mean *too much*.
Example: It is too hot in here.

The word *two* means the number *2*.

1. Complete each sentence by writing *to* or *too*.

a) Mom will drive us _____ the park.

b) I found a dime, and I found a quarter, _____.

c) I like _____ ride my new bike.

d) The soup is _____ hot to eat.

e) Terry is going _____ jump over the log.

f) Leon was hungry, and Akira was hungry, _____.

2. Write *to*, *too,* or *two* in the correct place in each sentence.

a) I am going _____ eat _____ muffins.

b) They are _____ tired _____ play _____ games of soccer.

c) She gave _____ apples _____ the children.

d) We saw _____ squirrels, and we saw _____ frogs, _____.

Write the Correct Word

The pairs of words below **sound the same** but are **spelled differently**. Make sure you write the word you mean.

Words	Examples
here – a place	Put your coat **here**.
hear – what your ears do	I can **hear** birds chirping.
see – what your eyes do	I **see** clouds in the sky.
sea – an ocean	The ship sailed across the **sea**.
right – correct, or the opposite of left	That is the **right** answer. I hurt my **right** foot.
write – make words on paper	She is going to **write** a story.

Circle the **correct word** in the brackets.

a) I know the (right   write) answer to the next question.

b) The (see   sea) had big waves during the storm.

c) The man told us to turn (right   write) at the next corner.

d) Do not leave your wet boots (here   hear).

e) My little brother can (right   write) his name.

f) Did you (see   sea) the rainbow this morning?

g) I could not (here   hear) what she said.

h) You were (right   write) when you said to turn (right   write).

i) We can (see   sea) the (see   sea) from (here   hear).

Canadian Grammar Practice 3 © Chalkboard Publishing

Correcting Errors: "The Lost Mitten"

Find and correct **eight** errors in the story below.

I could not find one of my blue mittens. I asked my brother and my sister. I asked my

parents. No one had seen my mitten. Where was it.

I looked all over the house. I looked in my bedroom. I looked in my sisters

bedroom. I looked in the kitchen and the living room, to. I could not find it. The blue

mitten was lost.

I felt sad I loved my blue mittens. I had too other pairs of mittens, but the blue

mittens were the warmer. I put on my green mittens. Then I went to say goodbye to our

cat. I always say goodbye to freddy before I go to school.

Freddy was asleep on a chair. Can you guess what I found under Freddys' paw?

I found my blue mitten!

Correcting Errors: "Owls"

Find and correct **ten** errors in the article below.

1   Owls are big birds. An owls feathers can be grey, brown, or white. You can find owls in

the United states, canada, and many other countries around the world.

2   Have you ever seen an owl. You will not see an owl during the day. Thats

because owls sleep during the day. They wake up to hunt at night.

3   Owls are good hunters they can here very soft sounds. Owls have large eyes

that can sea at night, and they have strong, sharp claws, two. Owls hunt frogs, mouses,

bugs, and birds.

Vocabulary List 1

---

resident

(*noun*) someone who lives in a certain place or building

*Example: I know many of the **residents** in my apartment building.*

---

convince

(*verb*) to make someone believe that something is true, or to make someone agree to do something

*Examples: I **convinced** Leo that my pet snake will not bite him.*
*I will **convince** Tammy to lend me her bike.*

---

ancient

(*adjective*) very old, or from a time that was long ago

*Example: This **ancient** coin was made 1000 years ago.*

---

purpose

(*noun*) the reason for doing something

*Example: Our **purpose** for cleaning out the basement was to get rid of things we do not need anymore.*

---

recall

(*verb*) to remember something

*Example: I know that woman, but I cannot **recall** where I met her.*

Vocabulary List 1 (continued)

In each sentence, write the **correct word** from the vocabulary list. For **verbs**, remember to use the correct **form** and **tense** (past, present, or future).

a) Janelle thought I was lying, so I _____ her that I was telling the truth.

b) Discovering new lands was the _____ of the explorers' journey.

c) I now live in Alberta, so I am not a _____ of Manitoba anymore.

d) I wish I could _____ the name of the restaurant where we ate last week.

e) The scientists were excited to find _____ dinosaur bones buried underground.

f) We tried to _____ Mom to let us stay up late so we could watch the rest of the movie.

g) One _____ in our apartment building always climbs the stairs instead of using the elevator.

h) The _____ of wearing mittens or gloves is to keep your hands warm.

i) Do you _____ that time when we rode on the roller coaster at the amusement park?

j) If you would like to come to the museum with us, we can see many

_____ objects.

Vocabulary List 1: Review

Vocabulary words: resident   convince   ancient   purpose   recall

1. Write the correct **vocabulary word** beside each definition.

   a) _____ : the reason for doing something

   b) _____ : to make someone agree to do something

   c) _____ : someone who lives in a certain place or building

   d) _____ : very old, or from a time that was long ago

   e) _____ : to remember something

2. Write the **correct** vocabulary word in each sentence. For **verbs**, remember to use the correct **form** and **tense** (past, present, or future).

   a) The _____ of wearing sunscreen is to make sure you do not get a sunburn.

   b) Yesterday, I _____ where I had put my book about secret codes.

   c) Jake is a great pitcher, so I am glad you _____ him to join our baseball team.

   d) When I was a _____ of this apartment building, I lived on the third floor.

   e) My parents thought I was too young to look after a puppy, so I had to

   _____ them I could do it.

   f) This _____ bowl was made 2000 years ago.

Vocabulary List 2

---

vehicle

(*noun*) a machine that carries people or things from one place to another

*Example: Cars, trucks, buses, and motorcycles are examples of **vehicles**.*

---

observe

(*verb*) to carefully watch (and sometimes listen to)

*Example: The scientist will **observe** the birds to see how they build their nest.*

---

predict

(*verb*) to say or think what will happen in the future

*Example: I see dark clouds in the sky, so I **predict** it will rain soon.*

---

annual

(*adjective*) happening once a year

*Example: Our city's **annual** winter festival happens every January.*

---

signal

(*noun*) something such as a body movement, light, or sound that sends a message

*Example: The sound of the fire alarm is a **signal** that you should leave the building.*

(*verb*) to send a message by using a body movement, light, or sound

*Example: A red traffic light **signals** drivers that they need to stop.*

Vocabulary List 2 (continued)

In each sentence, write the **correct word** from the vocabulary list. For **verbs**, remember to use the correct **form** and **tense** (past, present, or future).

a) A fire truck's siren is a _____ that drivers need to pull over to the side of the road.

b) At the magic show yesterday, I _____ the magician to see if I could find out how he did his tricks.

c) Someone who has a _____ large enough for seven people will give us a ride to the zoo.

d) Every July, we go to Chicago for our _____ visit with Uncle Frank and Aunt Judy.

e) Our team is three goals ahead, so I _____ that we will win the game.

f) The traffic lights are broken, so a police officer _____ to cars when they should go or stop.

g) A motorcycle is a _____ that can carry only one or two people.

h) I _____ that my parents will give me a new baseball glove for my birthday because they know I need one.

i) When the coach blows her whistle, it's a _____ that we should stop and listen to what she has to say.

j) For a week, the detective _____ the woman to find out where she went.

k) Your birthday is an _____ event.

Vocabulary List 2: Review

Vocabulary words: vehicle observe predict annual signal

1. Write the correct **vocabulary word** beside each definition.

   a) _____: something such as a body movement, light, or sound that sends a message

   b) _____: happening once a year

   c) _____: a machine that carries people or things from one place to another

   d) _____: to say or think what will happen in the future

   e) _____: to send a message by using a body movement, light, or sound

   f) _____: to carefully watch (and sometimes listen to)

2. Write the **correct** vocabulary word in each sentence. For **verbs**, remember to use the correct **form** and **tense** (past, present, or future).

   a) I studied hard for the test, so I _____ that I will get a good mark.

   b) A bus is a _____ that can carry a large number of people.

   c) We go on our _____ family vacation every August.

   d) Students usually raise their hand to _____ that they have a question.

   e) The parents _____ their children to make sure they took turns playing on the swings.

   f) The beeping of my alarm clock is a _____ that it is time to get up.

Vocabulary List 3

device

(*noun*) something that has been made to do a certain job

*Example: A shovel is a **device** people use to move dirt and snow.*

prevent

(*verb*) to stop something from happening

*Example: Putting on sunscreen can **prevent** you from getting a sunburn.*

attempt

(*noun*) a try at doing something

*Example: The batter's first **attempt** to hit the baseball was a strike.*

(*verb*) to try to do something

*Example: This box might be too heavy for me, but I will **attempt** to lift it.*

actual

(*adjective*) real or correct

*Examples: This toy giraffe is much shorter than an **actual** giraffe.*
*I thought the time was 1:00 p.m., but the **actual** time was 1:30 p.m.*

rarely

(*adverb*) not very often

*Example: Where we live, it **rarely** snows in April.*

Vocabulary List 3 (continued)

In each sentence, write the **correct word** from the vocabulary list. For **verbs**, remember to use the correct **form** and **tense** (past, present, or future).

a) I fell quite a few times because it was my first _____ at skating.

b) It _____ rains in the desert, so not many plants can grow there.

c) A nail clipper is a _____ that people use to cut their fingernails and toenails.

d) This movie about George Washington is based on _____ events that happened in his life.

e) A bicycle helmet can _____ you from hurting your head if you fall.

f) The cat _____ to catch the mouse, but the mouse was too fast.

g) Kate _____ reads poems because she likes reading stories better.

h) I thought the movie would be about an hour and a half long, but its

_____ length was two hours.

i) We put a fence around the backyard to _____ our dog from running out into the street.

j) A smoke detector is a _____ that tells people a fire might have started.

Vocabulary List 3: Review

Vocabulary words: device   attempt   prevent   actual   rarely

1. Write the correct **vocabulary word** beside each definition.

   a) _____: to try to do something

   b) _____: not very often

   c) _____: to stop something from happening

   d) _____: something that has been made to do a certain job

   e) _____: real or correct

   f) _____: a try at doing something

2. Write the **correct** vocabulary word in each sentence. For **verbs**, remember to use the correct **form** and **tense** (past, present, or future).

   a) An umbrella will _____ you from getting wet.

   b) She did not get the basketball in the hoop the first time she tried, but the

   ball did go in on her second _____.

   c) A microwave is a _____ that heats food quickly.

   d) It rained so much last summer that I _____ had to water the garden.

   e) The museum has only a copy of the old treasure map because the

   _____ map got lost.

Vocabulary List 4

arrange

(*verb*) to put in a neat, attractive, or proper order; to organize or make plans for

*Example: My mother **arranged** the flowers nicely in the vase.*

---

brief

(*adjective*) lasting only a short time

*Example: The butterfly sat on my arm only for a **brief** moment.*

---

cling

(*verb*) to hold on tightly to something

*Example: Tree frogs have sticky pads on their feet that help them **cling** to surfaces.*

---

crumple

(*verb*) to crush something so it becomes wrinkled and creased

*Example: Max was unhappy with his story, so he **crumpled** it up and threw it out.*

---

gradual

(*adjective*) taking place or progressing slowly or by degrees

*Example: In spring, there is a **gradual** change as the trees and flowers start to grow.*

---

swift

(*adjective*) happening quickly or immediately

*Example: The **swift** squirrel snatched the peanut and raced away with it.*

(*adverb*) describing something that moves quickly

*Example: The river is **swiftly** moving above the falls.*

Vocabulary List 4 (continued)

In each sentence, write the **correct word** from the vocabulary list. For **verbs**, remember to use the correct **form** and **tense** (past, present, or future).

a) The woman carefully placed her folded clothes in her suitcase, so they would not get

_____.

b) In one _____ move, the dog knocked the cup of water off the table and all over the floor.

c) I wish I could get taller fast, but I know it is a very _____ process.

d) Our cat got scared by the dog's sudden barking, so she is now _____ to the curtains.

e) My grandmother always _____ the candies on my cake to spell "Happy Birthday!"

f) The candle made a _____ sputtering sound before the flame went out.

g) That young man _____ served his customers at the restaurant.

h) The packing peanuts from the shipping box are _____ to my cat's fur.

i) The change in the baby's eye colour was so _____ that we only saw the difference in photos.

j) The neighbour's dog stopped barking for one _____ minute before he started all over again.

k) The scrap metal dealer _____ to pick up the old rusty car.

Vocabulary List 4: Review

Vocabulary words: arrange   brief   cling   crumple   gradual   swift

1. Write the correct **vocabulary word** beside each definition.

   a) _____ : taking place or progressing slowly

   b) _____ : happening quickly or immediately

   c) _____ : to put in a neat, attractive, or proper order

   d) _____ : to hold on tightly to something

   e) _____ : to crush, crease, and wrinkle something

   f) _____ : describing something that moves quickly

2. Write the **correct** vocabulary word in each sentence. For **verbs**, remember to use the correct **form** and **tense** (past, present, or future).

   a) Many people complain that spring and summer are too _____ in Canada.

   b) After the accident, my uncle made _____ progress in learning to walk again.

   c) Our dog is very _____ at escaping from my little brother's hugs.

   d) I sat on my new dress the wrong way and the skirt part got all _____.

   e) Aunt Amy whispered that she is _____ a party for my Uncle Ben for next weekend.

   f) The kind knight was _____ in moving to help the woman who had fallen.

Vocabulary List 5

avoid

(*verb*) to keep away from something, or stop oneself from doing something

*Example: The traffic report warned people to **avoid** Mill Street because it was flooded.*

---

clever

(*adjective*) smart; quick to learn, understand, or come up with ideas

*Example: My teacher said my idea for a mouse maze was very **clever**.*

---

doze

(*verb*) to sleep lightly

*Example: My grandfather always **dozes** off while watching television.*

---

flutter

(*verb*) to fly unsteadily or hover by flapping wings quickly and lightly

*Example: The little bird **fluttered** its wings while trying to land on the swaying branch.*

---

marsh

(*noun*) an area of land that is always very wet; a wetland

*Example: Frogs, turtles, beavers, and muskrats live among the cattails in the **marsh**.*

---

risk

(*noun*) a situation involving exposure to danger

*Example: The thief took a big **risk** by trying to sneak past the sleeping dog.*

(*verb*) to expose someone or something to danger, harm, or loss

*Example: Jack **risked** dropping the glass when he picked it up with his wet hands.*

Vocabulary List 5 (continued)

In each sentence, write the **correct word** from the vocabulary list. For **verbs**, remember to use the correct **form** and **tense** (past, present, or future).

a) My uncle, my father, and I went to see the tadpoles in the _____.

b) The old bridge is worn out, so you should not _____ walking across it.

c) Our pet rat is very _____. He has learned to do several tricks.

d) My baby sister is finally asleep, so we have to _____ making too much noise.

e) The girl was relaxing in the hammock, and slowly _____ off.

f) The butterfly was _____ its wings as it tried to land on the flower.

g) The people urged the mayor to protect the _____ where the ducks nest every year.

h) The girl took the _____ of hurting her feet when she wore flipflops on the hike.

i) My mother learned a _____ new way of folding napkins to make swans.

j) My brother can be lazy sometimes. He often tries to _____ doing his chores.

k) My cousin's cat _____ on the window sill in the sunshine this morning.

 Canadian Grammar Practice 3 © Chalkboard Publishing

Vocabulary List 5: Review

Vocabulary words: avoid clever doze flutter marsh risk

1. Write the correct **vocabulary word** beside each definition.

   a) _____ : to fly unsteadily by flapping wings quickly

   b) _____ : to keep away from something

   c) _____ : a situation involving exposure to danger

   d) _____ : an area of land that is always very wet

   e) _____ : to sleep lightly

   f) _____ : smart

   g) _____ : to expose to danger

2. Write the **correct** vocabulary word in each sentence. For **verbs**, remember to use the correct **form** and **tense** (past, present, or future).

   a) The bird _____ its wings while it ate the baby spiders off the window.

   b) I want to _____ looking bad, so I will not cut my own hair.

   c) On Saturdays, I often stay in bed late and _____ a little longer.

   d) Macy knew Robbie would tease her, so she _____ him in at recess.

   e) I found a _____ new way to tie my shoelaces.

   f) My brother took a _____ and asked Cara to the dance.

   g) The town held a weekend event to clean up the _____.

Grammar Review Test Grade 3

1. Underline all the **nouns** in each sentence.

   a) The dog plays with the tennis ball in the park.

   b) Most children enjoy making paintings with their fingers.

   c) My uncle used a hammer and nails to fix the shed.

   d) Kittens and puppies are popular pets for families with children.

   e) Marco decided to play soccer instead of playing baseball.

2. Write the **plural** of each noun.

   a) bunch _____

   b) child _____

   c) puppy _____

   d) zero _____

   e) fox _____

   f) elf _____

   g) potato _____

   h) photo _____

   i) berry _____

   j) scarf _____

3. In each sentence, circle the correct **possessive noun**. Think about whether the sentence needs a **singular** or **plural** possessive noun.

   a) My (brothers'   brother's) bicycles are all too small for them now.

   b) The (officer's   officers') lights were flashing.

   c) My three (hamsters'   hamster's) favourite hiding place is this box.

   d) This (Sundays'   Sunday's) class was about being kind to others.

        Canadian Grammar Practice 3 © Chalkboard Publishing

4. Rewrite each sentence. Use a **pronoun** to replace each **underlined word** or **group of words**.

a) Karen hopes that <u>Karen</u> can go camping with <u>her cousins</u> this summer.

_____

b) <u>My family and I</u> are going to the zoo tomorrow with <u>my aunt</u>.

_____

c) <u>The happy puppies</u> played with <u>the little boy</u>.

_____

5. In each sentence, write the correct **possessive pronoun** to replace the word or words in brackets.

a) Ravi is moving to Nova Scotia with _____ family. (Ravi's)

b) _____ note was taped to _____ door. (Mom's; the fridge's)

c) The boys met _____ favourite baseball player. (the boys')

6. Rewrite each sentence. Replace the **underlined words** with a **possessive pronoun**.

a) <u>Her book is</u> heavier than <u>my book</u>.

_____

b) <u>Your mittens</u> are more <u>colourful</u> than <u>their mittens</u>.

_____

c) <u>The firefighters'</u> bell is as loud as <u>the church's</u> bell.

_____

7. Circle each **adjective** and underline each **noun**. Draw an arrow from each **adjective** to the **noun** it describes.

   a) I wanted to watch another movie, but everyone was tired.

   b) Sonny barbecued delicious burgers for dinner.

   c) The young squirrels are playful today.

   d) Bright lightning lit up the stormy sky.

8. In each sentence, circle the correct way to use **adjectives** to compare.

   a) All the men were strong, but Little Mike was (stronger   the strongest).

   b) This tree is tall, but that tree is (taller   the tallest).

   c) All the dogs at the dog show were pretty, but my dog is (prettier   the prettiest).

9. In each sentence, circle the correct way to **compare** two or more things.

   a) Todd studied a lot, but his sister studied (more   the most).

   b) Ana and Hans was tired after the hike, but Terry was (more   the most) tired.

   c) Kai is (more   the most) flexible person in gymnastics class.

10. Complete the sentences with the correct word—*a*, **an**, or **the**.

   a) _____ spider and _____ octopus look a bit alike.

   b) In _____ store, we saw _____ ant farm.

   c) If you cut _____ apple through the middle, you will see _____ star inside.

   d) It is amazing how _____ cat and _____ dog are such good friends.

Canadian Grammar Practice 3 © Chalkboard Publishing

11. Circle all the **verbs** in each sentence.

   a) The players kicked and passed the soccer balls around the field.

   b) Mom and I mixed the cookie dough, then baked the cookies.

   c) We pulled the weeds, planted the flowers, then watered the garden.

   d) Making pizza and laughing with my family are two of my favourite activities.

12. Write the correct **present tense** form of the verb in brackets. (The present tense tells about actions that are happening **now**.)

   a) Yu _____ her bed every morning. (make)

   b) The baker _____ the dough to make the bread. (mix)

   c) A chick _____ its way out of its shell. (peck)

13. Write the correct **past tense** form of the verb in brackets. (The past tense tells about actions that have **already happened**.)

   a) Ted _____ his mother if Aaron could stay for dinner. (ask)

   b) My dad _____ all the laundry this weekend. (wash)

   c) Rani _____ some muffins at the school bake sale. (buy).

14. Write the correct **future tense** form of the verb in brackets. (The future tense tells about actions that will happen **in the future**.) Remember to use a **helping verb**.

   a) On Saturday, I _____ to my cousin's party. (go)

   b) My brother and I _____ some nice presents for our grandparents. (make)

   c) Katy and Tim _____ to the store to buy bread. (walk)

   d) Mom _____ my name in my jacket so I will not lose it. (stitch)

15. Circle the **linking** verbs and underline the **action** verbs.

   a) I lost my dime, but I found a quarter.

   b) We are all hungry for pizza.

   c) This jacket is my favourite.

   d) Kathy folded her paper and tucked it in her notebook.

16. Circle each **helping verb** and underline each **main verb**.

   a) All of us are going to the fair this weekend.

   b) My teacher will run in a marathon tomorrow.

   c) My class is excited about the field trip.

   d) When my dog is hungry, he drools.

17. Write the correct form of the **verb** in brackets. Make sure the subject and the verb **agree**.

   a) The ponies _____ around the field. (runs)

   b) Kerry _____ all the floors in the house. (sweep)

   c) The sky turns dark and lightning _____. (flash)

   d) The bird _____ to its nest. (fly)

   e) The pink paper _____ easier. (rip)

18. Circle the correct **helping verb** in brackets to tell about an action that has **already happened**.

   a) My brother (was   is   were) helping my dad mow the lawn.

   b) She (had   has) worked for most of her life.

   c) Our cousins (is   are   were) all coming over for a barbecue today.

   d) Those (are was   were) my favourite pair of jeans.

19. Circle the **adverbs** that describe **how**, **when**, **where**, **or how often** an action happens.

a) Mary always brushes her teeth after meals.

b) Theo takes out the garbage on Tuesdays.

c) The birds dropped seeds everywhere.

d) Victor shouted to Hans loudly.

e) Our uncle's dog rarely barks.

20. Add the correct **punctuation mark** (period, exclamation mark, or question mark) at the end of the sentence. Then tell **what kind** of sentence it is (telling, question, strong feeling, or command).

a) I can finally reach it___   _____

b) I want to watch this___   _____

c) Can you tell the time___   _____

d) Marcel just came home___   _____

e) Help me set the table___   _____

21. In each sentence, write the **contraction** for the words in brackets.

a) _____ sunny and hot out today. (It is)

b) _____ hurt yourself if you jump that far. (You will)

c) I told my mother _____ leaving for school now. (I am)

d) _____ coming over this afternoon. (They are)

e) Kelly said _____ going to move away soon. (she is)

Achievement Award – Canadian Grammar Practice Grade 3

GREAT WORK!

_____
NAME

Achievement Award – Canadian Grammar Practice Grade 3

GREAT GRAMMAR!

_____
NAME

Answers

What Is a Noun? p. 2

1. Tom, girl, man, Maria, grandfather, doctor

2. school, library, backyard, mall, beach, Canada

3. lamp, pencil, coat, car, tree

4. a) shoe, carrot, basement **b)** teacher, bed **c)** baby, sister, bedroom

5. a) kitchen **b)** Carlos, street **c)** truck, house **d)** Mom, bathroom

6. Answers will vary. Ensure the sentence includes three nouns.

7. Answers will vary. Ensure the sentence includes a person and a place.

8. Answers will vary. Ensure the sentence includes a person, a place, and a thing.

Make a Noun Collage, p. 3

You may wish to make a bulletin board display of children's collages.

What Are Proper Nouns? p. 4

1. b) New Year's Day

Answers to all other questions on this page will vary. Ensure that proper nouns start with a capital letter.

Making Nouns Plural, p. 5

1. a) dishes **b)** bunnies **c)** bushes **d)** boxes **e)** wishes **f)** matches

2. a) I got scratches on my arms. **b)** I saw ladies wearing dresses.

Tricky Plural Nouns, pp. 6–8

1. a) patios **b)** zeros **c)** tomatoes **d)** pianos

2. a) The heroes turned on radios to hear the news. **b)** Larry sent me photos of potatoes from his garden. **c)** In the videos, people heard echoes.

3. a) halves **b)** thieves **c)** wolves **d)** shelves

4. a) The chefs made loaves of bread **b)** Leaves blew onto the roofs. **c)** It is dangerous to play near cliffs. **d)** The sheriffs caught thieves.

5. a) knives **b)** fish **c)** lives **d)** sheep

6. a) The wives made lots of food for the party. **b)** Mice ran over my feet! **c)** The children fed the geese. **d)** The women saw deer in the woods.

Nouns Review Quiz, pp. 9–10

1. a) person, place, thing **b)** proper

2. a) Mom, mittens, shelf, closet **b)** Bees, butterflies, flowers, backyard **c)** mountains, British Columbia **d)** nurse, doctor, papers **e)** windows, bird, house **f)** Darnell, beach, friends

3. a) Mrs. Greenway, Tuesday **b)** Rover, Nova Scotia **c)** Dr. Conway, Labour Day **d)** Toronto, Canada **e)** Uncle Alfred, Florida **f)** Valentine's Day, February

4. a) boxes **b)** people **c)** videos **d)** lunches **e)** keys **f)** tomatoes **g)** babies **h)** wolves **i)** deer **j)** mice **k)** brushes **l)** shelves **m)** knives **n)** geese

5. a) sleeves **b)** videos **c)** children **d)** echoes **e)** roofs **f)** teeth **g)** tomatoes **h)** ponies

Singular Possessive Nouns, p. 11

1. a) Amira's **b)** bird's **c)** Omar's **d)** woman's

2. a) Mario turned the book's pages. **b)** The mug's handle broke off. **c)** The plant's leaves turned brown.

Plural Possessive Nouns, p. 12

1. a) sisters' **b)** cousins' **c)** cars' **d)** lions'

2. a) people's **b)** children's **c)** men's **d)** women's

More Practice with Possessive Nouns, pp. 13–14

1. a) My bike's front tire is flat. **b)** Please give me the store's phone number. **c)** Did you find Suki's pencil? **d)** This is my father's watch. **e)** The elephant's feet are huge!

2. a) The trees' leaves change colour in the fall. **b)** The jars' lids are in the top drawer. **c)** The people's cars are parked outside. **d)** My brothers' coats are in the closet. **e)** We could hear the women's voices.

Possessive Nouns Review Quiz, pp. 15–16

1. a) shirt's **b)** puppies' **c)** children's **d)** Kim's **e)** shoes' **f)** team's **g)** Kayla's

2. a) Underline "plant's," cross it out, and write "plants' " above it. **b)** Underline "bird's" and put a check mark above it. **c)** Underline "Liams'," cross it out, and write "Liam's" above it. **d)** Underline "sister's," cross it out, and write "sisters' " above it. **e)** Underline "Jeremy's" and put a check mark above it; underline "coats'," cross it out, and write "coat's" above it. **f)** Underline "womens'," cross it out, and write "women's" above it; underline "men's" and put a check mark above it. **g)** Underline "markers' " and put a check mark above it.

3. a) aunt's b) monkey's c) dog's d) cat's e) Jim's f) girl's g) team's

4. a) children's b) Scouts' c) women's d) clouds' e) people's f) men's g) racers'

Pronouns for People, p. 17

1. a) He **b)** They **c)** them

2. a) They played with the puppies. **b)** She showed the picture to him. **c)** They smiled at us. **d)** We waved goodbye to them.

Pronouns for Things, p. 18

1. a) it **b)** They **c)** them **d)** They

2. a) They gave them to us. **b)** They are too big for them to carry. **c)** We sent it to him. **d)** Will they sing for them?

Possessive Pronouns, pp. 19–20

1. a) my **b)** his **c)** their **d)** your **e)** My, our **f)** its **g)** her **h)** Our, their

2. a) Frank scratched his nose because it was itchy. **b)** We are going to have dinner at her house. **c)** The Smiths saw birds eating from their bird feeder. **d)** Its batteries are dead. **e)** "Emilio, is it your birthday today?" Gary asked. **f)** The teachers said, "It is our job to help you learn." **g)** Gail said, "You can borrow my eraser." **h)** The toy truck is missing one of its wheels.

More Possessive Pronouns, p. 21

1. a) Underline "his"; circle "mine." **b)** Underline "her"; circle "his." **c)** Circle "Yours" and "hers." **d)** Underline "their"; circle "ours" and "theirs." **e)** Circle "Hers" and "his."

Question at bottom of page: The possessive pronoun "his" sometimes comes before a noun and sometimes does not in these questions. Look at sentences (a) and (b).

2. a) My brother's feet are bigger than mine. **b)** Our dog barks louder than theirs. **c)** I think your joke is funnier than his. **d)** Are these hers or his?

3. a) our, theirs **b)** Your, mine **c)** My, yours **d)** ours **e)** mine, mine, hers **f)** your, theirs

Pronouns Review Quiz, pp. 23–24

1. a) My name is Eddie, and I can help you. **b)** We worked hard on our project. **c)** Please put them in the freezer. **d)** They gave him a birthday card. **e)** She has already returned them to us. **f)** They are too big for her. **g)** It is not too hard for them to read. **h)** He gave one apple to each of them.

2. a) His **b)** her, its **c)** their **d)** My **e)** Our **f)** Your **g)** their

3. a) Yours are longer than mine. **b)** His can jump farther than hers. **c)** Ours is on a higher floor than theirs. **d)** Hers is messier than mine.

What Is an Adjective? pp. 25–26

1. a) Circle "brown" and underline "mouse." **b)** Circle "large" and underline "book." **c)** Circle "scary" and underline "dragon." **d)** Circle "playful" and underline "puppy." **e)** Circle "green" and underline "mug." **f)** Circle "slippery" and underline "ice." **g)** Circle "loud" and underline "thunder." **h)** Circle "interesting" and underline "movie." **i)** Circle "funny" and underline "joke." **j)** Circle "round" and underline "table." **k)** Circle "tall" and underline "mountain." **l)** Circle "dirty" and underline "dishes." **m)** Circle "lonely" and underline "road." **n)** Circle "tall" and underline "grass." **o)** Circle "happy" and underline "dance." **p)** Circle "colourful" and underline "pigeons." **q)** Circle "angry" and underline "cat."

2. Sample answers: **a)** blue, new, warm **b)** loud, soft, clear **c)** dark, white, fluffy **d)** fast, quick, strong **e)** colourful, pretty, pink **f)** white, fat, hungry **g)** sleeping, lazy, tired

3. a) heavy **b)** warm **c)** bright **d)** great **e)** favourite **f)** sleepy, warm **g)** pretty, dark

Adjectives Before and After Nouns, p. 27

1. a) Circle "funny" and underline "clown." **b)** Circle "red" and underline "light." **c)** Circle "angry" and underline "woman." **d)** Circle "dry" and underline "towels." **e)** Circle "exciting" and underline "video." **f)** Circle "soft" and underline "pillow." **g)** Circle "cute" and underline "baby." **h)** Circle "delicious" and underline "sandwiches." **i)** Circle "bright" and underline "sun." **j)** Circle "cold" and underline "water." **k)** Circle "tired" and underline "Enzo." **l)** Circle "correct" and underline "answer."

2. a) Circle "huge" and underline "dinosaur"; draw an arrow from "huge" to "dinosaur." Circle "sharp" and underline "teeth"; draw an arrow from "sharp" to "teeth." **b)** Circle "happy" and underline "children"; draw an arrow from "happy" to "children." Circle "colourful" and underline "rainbow"; draw an arrow from "colourful" to "rainbow." **c)** Circle "tall" and underline "woman"; draw an arrow from "tall" to "woman." Circle "leaky" and underline "roof"; draw an arrow from "leaky" to "roof."

Adjectives Can Describe How Many, p. 28

1. a) Circle "three" and underline "apples"; draw an arrow from "three" to "apples." Underline "tree." **b)** Underline "Raj." Circle "four" and underline "coins"; draw an arrow from "four" to "coins." Underline "bed." **c)** Underline "Sandra." Circle "two" and underline "squirrels"; draw an arrow from "two" to "squirrels." Underline "tree." **d)** Circle "eight" and underline "frogs"; draw an arrow from "eight" to "frogs." Underline "pond."

2. a) several **b)** many **c)** Few **d)** some **e)** many, few **f)** several, many

Using Adjectives to Compare Two Things, p. 29

1. a) older **b)** thicker **c)** smaller **d)** colder **e)** brighter **f)** warmer **g)** softer

2. a) sadder **b)** hotter **c)** fatter **d)** bigger

Using Adjectives to Compare More Than Two Things, p. 30

1. a) fastest; runners in the race **b)** coldest; days of the year **c)** warmest; all the coats **d)** softest; all the beds

2. a) the cleanest **b)** the brightest **c)** the thickest **d)** the smallest

Tricky Adjectives That Compare, p. 31

a) better; two things **b)** worse; two things **c)** the best; more than two things **d)** farther; two things **e)** the most; more than two things **f)** the worst; more than two things

Adjectives That Use *More* and *Most* to Compare, p. 32

1. a) more **b)** the most **c)** more **d)** the most **e)** more **f)** the most **g)** more **h)** the most

2. a) grumpiest **b)** hairier **c)** sillier **d)** curliest

Make an Adjective Poem, p. 33

You may wish to create a bulletin board display of children's poems.

Using the Articles *A*, *An*, and *The*, pp. 34–35

a) the **b)** a **c)** the **d)** an **e)** The **f)** a, the **g)** an, a **h)** a, a **i)** a, an **j)** the, the **k)** The, a, the **l)** the, the **m)** A, the, an

Adjectives and Articles Review Quiz, pp. 36–37

1. a) Circle "old," underline "man," and draw an arrow from "old" to "man"; circle "big," underline "house," and draw an arrow from "big" to "house"; circle "beautiful," underline "lake," and draw an arrow from "beautiful" to "lake." **b)** Circle "wet," underline "floor," and draw an arrow from "wet" to "floor"; circle "slippery" and draw an arrow from "slippery" to "floor." **c)** Underline "soup," circle "hot," and draw an arrow from "hot" to "soup"; circle "delicious" and draw an arrow from "delicious" to "soup." **d)** Circle "Two," underline "women," and draw an arrow from "Two" to "women"; underline "chairs"; circle "tall," underline "tree," and draw an arrow from "tall" to "tree." **e)** Circle "Many," underline "children," and draw an arrow from "Many" to "children"; circle "funny," underline "stories," and draw an arrow from "funny" to "stories"; circle "scary," underline "stories," and draw an arrow from "scary" to "stories." **f)** Circle "Several," underline "people," and draw an arrow from "Several" to "people"; circle "some," underline "snacks," and draw an arrow from "some" to "snacks"; underline "party." **g)** Circle "Few," underline "guests," and draw an arrow from "Few" to "guests"; circle "four," underline "people," and draw an arrow from "four" to "people." **h)** Circle "little," underline "boy," and draw an arrow from "little" to "boy"; circle "red," underline "hair," and draw an arrow from "red" to "hair"; circle "tired" and draw an arrow from "tired" to "boy."

2. a) faster **b)** the loudest **c)** longer **d)** shorter **e)** the tallest **f)** the hungriest **g)** funnier

3. a) more **b)** the most **c)** the most **d)** more **e)** the most **f)** more

4. a) a **b)** the **c)** a **d)** an **e)** a **f)** the **g)** an

What Is a Verb? p. 38

1. a) jumps **b)** flies **c)** gives **d)** flashes **e)** forgets **f)** sends **g)** see **h)** squeaks **i)** dance **j)** runs

2. a) tells, cleans **b)** writes, says **c)** builds, explores **d)** hears, hides **e)** buys, pours **f)** remembers, asks, scrubs **g)** skips, decides

Make a Verb Collage, p. 39

You may wish to make a bulletin board display of children's collages.

Canadian Grammar Practice 3 © Chalkboard Publishing

The Verbs *Be*, *Do*, and *Have*, pp. 40–41

1. a) is b) are c) am d) are
2. a) do b) does c) do d) does
3. a) have b) have c) has d) have
4. a) was b) had c) did d) had e) were, was f) had
5. a) was b) did c) had d) were e) had f) were

More Practice with *Be*, *Do*, and *Have*, pp. 42–43

1. a) past b) present c) past d) past e) present f) present g) past h) present i) present
2. a) was b) have c) did d) were e) am f) have g) did
3. a) was b) did c) have d) are e) had f) did g) are h) did i) has

Linking Verbs, pp. 44–45

1. a) Circle "were." b) Underline "ran." c) Circle "is." d) Circle "are." e) Underline "fell." f) Circle "am."
2. a) Underline "painted" and circle "is." b) Circle "are" and underline "eat." c) Circle "were" and underline "picked."
   d) Circle "am" and underline "build." e) Circle "is" and "was." f) Underline "slipped" and "fell." g) Circle "were"
   and underline "laughed." h) Circle "are" and underline "drew." i) Underline "swam" and circle "was." j) Circle
   "am" and "is."

Spelling Present Tense Verbs, p. 46

1. a) copies b) cries c) buys d) flies e) tries
2. a) scratches b) pushes c) passes d) mixes e) catches

Past Tense Verbs, p. 47

1. a) invented b) coughed c) shared d) worked e) borrowed f) escaped g) agreed h) exploded
2. a) chased b) chewed c) filled
3. a) past b) present c) present

Spelling Past Tense Verbs, p. 48

1. a) tripped b) stopped c) stirred d) dripped e) stepped
2. a) cried b) carried c) hurried d) worried e) scurried

Tricky Past Tense Verbs, pp. 49–50

1. a) had b) said c) ate d) came
2. a) We drive to the grocery store. b) The squirrel eats all the nuts. c) I have two pencils in my desk. d) Carly
comes to my house every week.
3. a) went b) drank c) thought d) bought
4. a) We drink juice with our breakfast. b) He buys a new toy for his grandson. c) Anna finds lots of seashells at
   the beach. d) I think about my best friend.

Future Tense Verbs, p. 51

1. a) will ride b) will swim c) will shine d) will drive
2. a) Timothy will plant a tree in the backyard. b) Carlos and Mary will talk about the movie. c) People will laugh at
   all my silly jokes.

Helping Verbs: Present and Future Tenses, pp. 52–53

1. **a)** Circle "is" and underline "looking." **b)** Circle "is" and underline "blowing." **c)** Circle "am" and underline "brushing." **d)** Circle "are" and underline "chasing." **e)** Circle "is" and underline "cutting." **f)** Circle "am" and underline "working." **g)** Circle "are" and underline "pulling." **h)** Circle "are" and underline "washing."

2. **a)** The children will plant tulips. **b)** We will hang the pictures on the wall. **c)** I will sing my favourite song. **d)** The birds will build a nest in the tree. **e)** They will ask the librarian some questions.

Helping Verbs: Past Tense, pp. 54–55

1. **a)** Circle "has" and underline "walked." **b)** Circle "had" and underline "chewed." **c)** Circle "have" and underline "grown." **d)** Circle "have" and underline "dropped." **e)** Circle "has" and underline "dried." **f)** Circle "had" and underline "stopped." **g)** Circle "have" and underline "wrapped." **h)** Circle "have" and underline "played." **i)** Circle "have" and underline "built." **j)** Circle "has" and underline "invited." k) Circle "had" and underline "melted."

2. **a)** was **b)** were **c)** were **d)** was **e)** was **f)** were

3. **a)** walked **b)** chirping **c)** climbing **d)** stirring **e)** collecting

Subject–Verb Agreement, pp. 56–57

1. **a)** runs **b)** glows **c)** sail **d)** grow **e)** scratches **f)** wish **g)** follows **h)** blow

2. **a)** studies **b)** falls **c)** unload **d)** brushes **e)** bury **f)** look

3. **a)** rushes **b)** watches **c)** say **d)** jumps **e)** sing **f)** creeps **g)** goes **h)** ride **i)** hisses

Pronoun–Verb Agreement, pp. 58–59

1. **a)** matches **b)** see **c)** fixes **d)** run **e)** count **f)** finds **g)** lend

2. **a)** kisses **b)** tie **c)** makes **d)** takes **e)** touches **f)** notice **g)** chew **h)** misses

3. **a)** keeps; a blanket **b)** make; batteries **c)** buzzes; alarm clock **d)** help; glasses **e)** goes; belt **f)** come; firefighters

Verbs Review Quiz 1, pp. 60–61

1. **a)** grow, cut **b)** cheers, hits **c)** climb, pick **d)** erased, wrote

2. **a)** make, tell, takes **b)** find, ask, sees **c)** write, listen, bring

3. **a)** does **b)** fixes **c)** catch **d)** flies **e)** buys **f)** misses **g)** am

4. **a)** walked **b)** clapped **c)** was **d)** carried **e)** finished **f)** drove **g)** bought **h)** knew **i)** were

5. **a)** will call **b)** will read **c)** will visit **d)** will grow **e)** will make

Verbs Review 2, pp. 62–63

1. **a)** Circle "was" and underline "found." **b)** Underline "read" and circle "are." **c)** Circle "were" and underline "told." **d)** Circle "was" and "were."

2. **a)** Circle "is" and underline "making." **b)** Circle "were" and underline "honking." **c)** Circle "am" and underline "running." **d)** Circle "are" and underline "singing."

3. **a)** climb **b)** uses **c)** has **d)** are **e)** find **f)** brushes

4. **a)** are **b)** is **c)** am **d)** are

5. **a)** The hungry lions will hunt for food. **b)** I will walk to the grocery store.

6. **a)** was **b)** had **c)** were **d)** has **e)** have **f)** were

Some Adverbs Describe How, p. 64

1. **a)** slowly **b)** quietly **c)** loudly **d)** carefully **e)** correctly **f)** gently

2. **a)** gracefully **b)** happily **c)** honestly **d)** sweetly **e)** tightly **f)** silently

Some Adverbs Describe When, p. 65

1. a) this afternoon **b)** next **c)** Tomorrow **d)** now **e)** soon **f)** at lunchtime **g)** Yesterday **h)** Next **i)** immediately

2. a) Later; later, sing **b)** next; next, swim **c)** Soon; soon, arrive

Some Adverbs Describe Where, p. 66

1. a) here: here, hang **b)** inside; inside, plays **c)** downstairs; downstairs, found **d)** there; there, put

2. a) everywhere **b)** away **c)** nearby **d)** anywhere **e)** somewhere

Some Adverbs Describe How Often, p. 67

1. a) always **b)** twice **c)** often **d)** never **e)** once

2. a) frequently **b)** constantly **c)** rarely **d)** usually **e)** seldom **f)** occasionally

Adverbs Review Quiz, pp. 68–69

1. a) cheerfully **b)** angrily **c)** correctly **d)** gently **e)** politely **f)** safely **g)** quietly

2. a) yesterday **b)** later **c)** soon **d)** now **e)** today **f)** next **g)** tomorrow **h)** late

3. a) here **b)** downstairs **c)** somewhere **d)** outside

4. a) always **b)** often **c)** never **d)** twice

5. a) how **b)** how often **c)** when **d)** where

Complete Subjects, p. 70

a) The sly fox **b)** Several silly clowns **c)** Many different types of seashells **d)** The lights of the city **e)** A large black bear **f)** My friend Jessica **g)** Many children in my class **h)** The people of the town **i)** Fire trucks and firefighters

Complete Predicates, p. 71

a) swims in our pool every day **b)** ate all my mother's lilies **c)** tumbled out of the box **d)** made peanut butter sandwiches **e)** read newspapers only on weekends **f)** painted my bedroom mint green today **g)** contains multiplication problems **h)** rolled all the way down the hill

What Comes at the End of a Sentence? pp. 72–73

1. a) question mark **b)** exclamation mark or period **c)** exclamation mark **d)** question mark **e)** period **f)** exclamation mark or period **g)** question mark

2. Ensure that children have written the correct kind of sentence for each section.

One Sentence or Two? p. 74

a) I like Lisa. She is my friend. **b)** Paul likes to run. He runs fast. **c)** It was raining. I got wet. **d)** Dad told a story. It was funny. **e)** The telephone rang. It woke me up.

Joining Sentences with *And* or *But*, p. 75

1. a) but **b)** and **c)** but **d)** and

2. a) The sun is shining, **and** it is a nice day. **b)** Hans watered the plant, **but** it died. **c)** I wore a warm coat, **but** I was still cold. **d)** Jana likes reading, **and** she reads often. **e)** Dad found his glasses, **but** he lost them again.

Joining Sentences with *Or* or *So*, p. 76

1. a) or **b)** or **c)** so **d)** so **e)** or

2. a) Her bike had a flat tire, **so** she walked to school. **b)** I might keep this photo, **or** I might give it to Stanley. **c)** Sandra might keep her hair long, **or** she might get it cut short. **d)** Mika had dirty hands, **so** he washed them.

Sentences and Punctuation Review Quiz, pp. 77–78

1. a) Add an exclamation mark; strong feeling b) Add a period; telling c) Add a period OR exclamation mark; command d) Add a question mark; question e) Add a period; telling f) Add a question mark; question

2. a) Tina is funny. She makes me laugh. b) Correct c) The sun was shining. It was a nice day. d) The dogs are barking. They make lots of noise.

3. a) Alan plays piano, and he practices every day. b) I was tired, but I did not go to bed. c) Laura does not like grapes, but she ate two, anyway. d) The phone rang, and Dad answered it. e) Wayne looks sick, but he said he feels fine.

4. a) so b) or c) so d) so e) or

What Is a Contraction? p. 79

1. a) they're b) I'm c) We're d) you're e) It's f) that's

2. a) She's going to be upset if he's late. b) I'm sure that's my notebook.

More Contractions, p. 80

1. a) We'll b) you'll c) she'll d) I'll e) They'll f) he'll

2. a) I will bring sandwiches, and you will bring juice. We will have a great picnic!

Abbreviations, pp. 81–82

1. a) Dr. b) road c) St. d) avenue e) Dr., doctor f) Rd. g) street h) Ave.

2. a) Dr. Greyson went to school with Mrs. Scott. b) Wilson Ave. is near Westside Park. c) How close is Tower Rd. to where Mr. Castle works? d) Are there lots of trees on your street?

Contractions and Abbreviations Review Quiz, pp. 83–84

1. a) he's b) it's c) We'll d) I'll e) That's f) you'll g) They're

2. a) she will b) I am c) We are d) they will e) you are f) She is g) he will h) They will

3. a) Dr. b) Mr. c) Ave. d) Rd.

4. a) You're going to be taller than your father. b) Mrs. Henderson thinks that's a wonderful idea. c) He's certain that Alfonso lives on this street. d) They're walking their dog along Wilson Rd. e) Western Ave. is closed because it's flooded.

Using *To, Too,* or *Two*, p. 85

1. a) to b) too c) to d) too e) to f) too

2. a) to, two b) too, to, two c) two, to d) two, two, too

Write the Correct Word, p. 86

a) right b) sea c) right d) here e) write f) see g) hear h) right, right i) see, sea, here

Correcting Errors: "The Lost Mitten," p. 87

Paragraph 1, sentence 5: Where was it?

Paragraph 2, sentence 3: I looked in my sister's bedroom.

Paragraph 2, sentence 4: I looked in the kitchen and the living room, too.

Paragraph 3, sentence 1: I felt sad. I loved my blue mittens.

Paragraph 3, sentence 2: I had two other pairs of mittens, but the blue mittens were the warmest.

Paragraph 3, sentence 5: I always say goodbye to Freddy before I go to school.

Paragraph 4, sentence 2: Can you guess what I found under Freddy's paw?

Correcting Errors: "Owls," p. 88

Paragraph 1, sentence 2: An <u>owl's</u> feathers can be grey, brown, or white.

Paragraph 1, sentence 3: You can find owls in the United <u>States</u>, <u>Canada</u>, and many other countries around the world.

Paragraph 2, sentence 1: Have you ever seen an <u>owl?</u>

Paragraph 2, sentence 3: <u>That's</u> because owls sleep during the day.

Paragraph 3, sentence 1: Owls are good <u>hunters. They</u> can <u>hear</u> very soft sounds.

Paragraph 3, sentence 2: Owls have large eyes that can <u>see</u> at night, and they have strong, sharp claws, <u>too</u>.

Paragraph 3, sentence 3: Owls hunt frogs, <u>mice</u>, bugs, and birds.

Vocabulary List 1, p. 90

a) convinced b) purpose c) resident d) recall e) ancient f) convince g) resident h) purpose i) recall j) ancient

Vocabulary List 1: Review, p. 91

1. a) purpose b) convince c) resident d) ancient e) recall
2. a) purpose b) recalled c) convinced d) resident e) convince f) ancient

Vocabulary List 2, p. 93

a) signal b) observed c) vehicle d) annual e) predict f) signals g) vehicle h) predict i) signal j) observed k) annual

Vocabulary List 2: Review, p. 94

1. a) signal b) annual c) vehicle d) predict e) signal f) observe
2. a) predict b) vehicle c) annual d) signal e) observed f) signal

Vocabulary List 3, p. 96

a) attempt b) rarely c) device d) actual e) prevent f) attempted g) rarely h) actual i) prevent j) device

Vocabulary List 3: Review, p. 97

1. a) attempt b) rarely c) prevent d) device e) actual f) attempt
2. a) prevent b) attempt c) device d) rarely e) actual

Vocabulary List 4, p. 99

a) crumpled b) swift c) gradual d) clinging e) arranges f) brief g) swiftly h) clinging i) gradual j) brief k) arranged

Vocabulary List 4: Review, p. 100

1. a) gradual b) swift c) arrange d) cling e) crumple f) swift
2. a) brief b) gradual c) swift d) crumpled e) arranging f) swift

Vocabulary List 5, p. 102

a) marsh b) risk c) clever d) avoid e) dozed f) fluttering g) marsh h) risk i) clever j) avoid k) dozed

Vocabulary List 5: Review, p. 103

1. a) fluttering b) avoid c) risk d) marsh e) doze f) clever g) risk
2. a) fluttered b) risk c) doze d) avoided e) clever f) risk g) marsh

1. **a)** dog, ball, park **b)** children, paintings, fingers **c)** uncle, hammer, nails, shed **d)** Kittens, puppies, pets, families, children **e)** Marco, soccer, baseball

2. **a)** bunches **b)** children **c)** puppies **d)** zeros **e)** foxes **f)** elves **g)** potatoes **h)** photos **i)** berries **j)** scarves

3. **a)** brothers' **b)** officer's **c)** hamsters' **d)** Sunday's

4. **a)** Karen hopes that <u>she</u> can go camping with <u>them</u> this summer. **b)** <u>We</u> are going to the zoo tomorrow with <u>her</u>. **c)** <u>They</u> played with <u>him</u>.

5. **a)** his **b)** her, its **c)** their

6. **a)** Hers is heavier than mine. **b)** Yours are more colourful than theirs. **c)** Their bell is as loud as its bell.

7. **a)** Circle "another" and underline "movie," draw an arrow from "another" to "movie"; circle "tired" and underline "everyone," draw an arrow from "tired" to "everyone." **b)** Circle "delicious" and underline "burgers," draw an arrow from "delicious" to "burgers." **c)** Circle "young" and underline "squirrels," draw an arrow from "young" to "squirrels"; circle "playful" and underline "squirrels," draw an arrow from "playful" to "squirrels." **d)** Circle "Bright" and underline "lightning," draw an arrow from "Bright" to "lightning"; circle "stormy" and underline "sky," draw an arrow from "stormy" to "sky."

8. **a)** the strongest **b)** taller **c)** the prettiest

9. **a)** more **b)** the most **c)** the most

10. **a)** A, a **b)** the, an **c)** an, a **d)** the, the

11. **a)** kicked, passed **b)** mixed, baked **c)** pulled, planted, watered **d)** Making, laughing

12. **a)** makes, **b)** mixes **c)** hatches

13. **a)** asked **b)** washed **c)** bought

14. **a)** will go **b)** will make **c)** will walk **d)** will stitch

15. **a)** underline "lost" and "found" **b)** circle "are" **c)** circle "is" **d)** underline "folded" and "tucked"

16. **a)** circle "are" and underline "going" **b)** circle "will" and underline "run" **c)** circle "is" and underline "excited" **d)** circle "is" and underline "hungry" and "drools"

17. **a)** run **b)** sweeps **c)** flashes **d)** flies **e)** rips

18. **a)** was **b)** had **c)** were **d)** were

19. **a)** always **b)** Tuesdays **c)** everywhere **d)** loudly **e)** rarely

20. **a)** exclamation mark, strong feeling **b)** period, telling **c)** question mark, question **d)** period, telling **e)** period, command

21. **a)** It's **b)** You'll **c)** I'm **d)** They're **e)** she's